The Past
The Road to Independence

THROUGH AFRICAN EYES

꙳ Volume 1

The Past
The Road to Independence

Leon E. Clark

THE APEX PRESS
ROWMAN & LITTLEFIELD PUBLISHERS, INC.
Lanham • Boulder • New York • Toronto • Plymouth, UK

THE APEX PRESS
Published by Rowman & Littlefield Publishers, Inc.
A wholly owned subsidiary of The Rowman & Littlefield Publishing Group, Inc.
4501 Forbes Boulevard, Suite 200, Lanham, Maryland 20706
www.rowman.com

10 Thornbury Road, Plymouth PL6 7PP, United Kingdom

Copyright © 1988, 1991 by Leon E. Clark

British Library Cataloguing in Publication Information Available

Library of Congress Cataloging-in-Publication Data
Clark, Leon E.
Through African Eyes.
Includes index.
Contents: v. 1. The past.
ISBN 13: 978-0-938960-27-0 (paperback)
    1.   Africa--History. [1. Africa] I. Title. II. Series
DT20.C54 1988
960   88-16720

Cover design by Rubin Krassner; photograph on page 8 by Leon E. Clark

⊖™ The paper used in this publication meets the minimum requirements of American National Standard for Information Sciences—Permanence of Paper for Printed Library Materials, ANSI/NISO Z39.48-1992.

Printed in the United States of America

To all Africans and their descendants throughout the world, who have given better than they have received.

About the Author

Leon E. Clark, is a faculty member at American University in Washington, D.C., where he directs a graduate program in International Education. He received his B.A. and M.A. from Yale University and his doctorate in International Education from the University of Massachusetts. For more than 20 years he has been involved in a variety of educational activities both within and outside the United States. He has been a high school teacher and curriculum specialist; associate director of the Social Sciences and Humanities Center, Teachers College, Columbia; education director of the Population Reference Bureau; and associate director of the Governmental Affairs Institute in Washington, D.C. He has also taught in the University of Mysore, India, and conducted research and development projects throughout Asia and Africa. In recent years he has specialized in nonformal education and training activities for rural development, working largely in West and East Africa but also in South Asia and the Middle East. The author of several books and numerous articles on education and international affairs, Dr. Clark serves as the general editor of the CITE World Culture Series.

Acknowledgments

The initial research for parts of this book began as early as 1967; the latest changes in the manuscript were made as recently as 1991. Over a period of more than 20 years, associations and contacts, ideas and directions, change dramatically and sometimes imperceptibly, leaving behind a vaguely defined but broad wake of indebtedness. It is impossible to thank by name everyone who has helped me in one way or another. But certain people stand out.

In the early stages of work, Richard Hull made several helpful suggestions about historical sources and themes, and Immanuel Wallerstein did the same for the section on nationalism. Colin Turnbull helped set the tone for the treatment of the colonial period, and Susan Hall found material to illustrate it.

More recently, I have benefited from the critical comments of Barry Beyer and from the support of two graduate students, Cristine Buckett and Ann Scholz, who not only reacted to my writing and choice of selections but also compiled the index for this volume. I am also indebted to Brenda Bryant for her sharp editing and her gentle hand-holding.

Finally, there are two people for whom the cliche "without whom it would have been impossible" fits. Ward Morehouse, president of the Council on International and Public Affairs, not only found the resources to finance the initial efforts that produced THROUGH AFRICAN EYES, but he has continued to follow the progress of the books and is the publisher of this new work.

My wife, Maria, has left her imprint on every aspect of this book, from the choice of verbs to the cropping of photographs. Her emotional support, as well as her goading encouragement, have kept me going more than she will ever know.

L.E.C.

Contents

Acknowledgements 7
Preface 11
Foreword: The Hands of the Blacks 15

Part I: THE AFRICAN PAST

Introduction 21
Ancient Ghana—Kingdom of Gold 27
The Kingdom of Mali 37
Griots: The Oral Tradition 47
Sun, Science and History 54
The Rise of Songhay 57
Ethiopia and East Africa 63

Part II: THE COMING OF THE EUROPEAN

Introduction 77
Slaves, Guns, More Slaves 80
The Story of a Slave 87
"Ivory First, Child Afterwards" 100
The Triangular Tempest 104
Ending the Slave Trade 109
Treaties for Trade 114

Part III: THE COLONIAL EXPERIENCE

Introduction 119
"Too White, Like a Devil" 123

That Was No Welcome, "That Was No Brother"   125
King Ja Ja, Business Whiz   131
The Coming of the Pink Cheeks   137
The Hut Tax War   148
Rhodes Steals "Rhodesia"   152
Leopold, the Janitor   162
White Man's Cotton   167
Ibrahimo Becomes a Christian   174
A Missionary Meets His Match   188
Anglo-Saxon Destiny   191
"Is There Anybody Here?" and Martyr   194

Part IV: THE RISE OF NATIONALISM: FREEDOM REGAINED

Introduction   201
The Parable of the Eagle   209
The New Politics   212
The Congo Wins Freedom   221
The African Outlook   227
Negritude   235
    "African Heart"   236
    "Africa"   236
    "Limbo"   238
Kenya: The Man and the Elephant   239
The "Mau Mau" Revolt   244
The Martyr   253
Reflections of a Leader   263
Independence Ledger   272

Sources   275
Index   279

Preface

People—and nations—have a tendency to look at the outside world from their own perspectives. This is natural and perhaps necessary, for we are all prisoners of a particular space and time. But how limiting and boring one perspective can be! And how faulty and biased our information can be if we listen only to ourselves!

The main goal of THROUGH AFRICAN EYES is to broaden our perspective by presenting a largely African view of Africa and the world. The hope is that by looking at Africa from the "inside" we will add balance to our predominantly "outside" and therefore lopsided view. In short, the hope is that looking through African eyes will mitigate the negative effects of our ethnocentrism.

Most of the selections in these books, then, have been written by Africans, and they come from a variety of sources: autobiographies, fiction, poetry, newspaper and magazine articles, radio broadcasts, letters, diaries, speeches and historical documents. (Each selection is identified by a bracketed number at the end of its INTRODUCTION, with all sources listed numerically at the end of the volume.)

Unlike traditional surveys or histories, THROUGH AFRICAN EYES does not try to "cover" all of Africa or to offer "expert" analysis by outside observers. Instead, it focuses on a few major themes and presents material that re-creates, as authentically and concretely as possible, the reality of African life. Interpretation is left to the reader. In effect, these books have two major goals: to let Africans speak for themselves, and to let readers think for themselves.

This does not mean, however, that scholarship has been relegated to a secondary position. Basic concepts and insights from history and the social sciences have been applied throughout in the selection of material. And the INTRODUCTION preceding each reading attempts to put the reading in historical and cultural context, referring, where relevant, to academic attitudes and debates surrounding the issues at hand. In addition, POSTSCRIPT commentaries and selections written especially for these books fill in gaps where they may exist between readings. But the overriding concern has been to *show* Africa rather to *explain* it, to present the concreteness of experience rather than the abstractness of detached analysis.

The first edition of THROUGH AFRICAN EYES consisted of six volumes organized around the themes of tradition, modernization, history, colonialism, nationalism and nation-building. This new edition, while dealing with some of these same themes, devotes more space to contemporary economic and political issues and contains substantially more material by and about African women. Essentially, this new edition is a new work. It is organized differently, has more than 50 percent new material, and is presented in two volumes instead of six. As before, THROUGH AFRICAN EYES focuses on Africa south of the Sahara, covering 46 of the continent's 52 nations. (North Africa is covered in THROUGH MIDDLE EASTERN EYES, another title in the CITE World Cultures Series.)

Volume 1 of the new THROUGH AFRICAN EYES—The Past: The Road to Independence—highlights major developments in African history from approximately 1,000 A.D. to the present, including extensive coverage of the colonial period and the independence movements that followed.

Volume 2—The Present: Tradition and Change—looks at modern Africa by examining contemporary cultural practices in the light of their traditional origins and the changes now taking place. It also explores the political and economic development challenges facing African nations today.

This volume, Vol. 1, has five parts, organized chronologically. Part I, "The African Past," attempts to convey some idea of the sophistication of early Africa, focusing on the ancient kingdoms of both West and East Africa. Part II, "The Coming of the European," lays bare the stark reality of the Atlantic slave trade and its impact on Africa. Part III, "The Colonial Experience," examines the effects of European control on the cultural, social, economic and political lives of Africans. Part IV, "The Rise of Nationalism: Freedom Regained," depicts the end of this control, brought about by the rise of African nationalism, which restored freedom to most of the continent.

In some ways, Africa may seem different from the West, and indeed it is. But in many more ways, the Africans as people are similar to people anywhere in the world. Human beings, no matter where they live, face the same basic needs: to eat, to work, to love, to play, to get along with other people and with their environments. Learning how Africans respond to these needs may teach us something useful for our own lives.

More importantly, getting to know Africans as people— sharing in their thoughts and feelings, their beliefs and aspirations—should help us to develop a sense of empathy, a feeling of identity, with human beings everywhere. In the end, we should know more about ourselves—indeed, we should have an expanded definition of who we are—because we will know more about the common humanity that all people share. Self-knowledge may be the ultimate justification for studying about other people.

Leon E. Clark

Washington, D.C.
January, 1988

Foreword:

The Hands of the Blacks

❧ INTRODUCTION: It seems appropriate to have an African write the Foreword to this book, and to have that Foreword set the tone for what follows. The story "The Hands of the Blacks" answers both demands admirably.

Set in the East African country of Mozambique when that country was still a colony of Portugal, this story depicts the experiences of a Mozambican boy as he grapples with the demeaning myths concocted to support racism. It is the story of only one youngster, but in a sense it portrays much of the history of colonial Africa—and of prejudice everywhere.

The author of this story, Luis Bernado Honwana, was imprisoned by the Portuguese for "political subversive activities" in 1966 when he was 24 years old. "The Hands of the Blacks" appeared a year later. Today Mozambique is independent and Luis Honwana is the Minister of Culture.

But the final liberation of Southern Africa is far from complete. While traveling in the United States in the summer of 1987, Luis Honwana received word that his wife's sister and her husband had been killed in a raid in the Mozambican capital of Maputo. The Mozambique government believes the attackers were South African commandos. The road to independence in southern Africa is still a rocky one.[1] ❧

I don't remember now how we got onto the subject, but one day teacher said that the palms of the blacks' hands were much lighter than the rest of their bodies because only a few centuries ago they walked around on all fours, like wild animals, so their palms weren't exposed to the sun, which went

* All selections are numbered sequentially; their sources are listed at the end of the volume.

15

on darkening the rest of their bodies. I thought of this when
Senhor Padre told us after catechism that we were absolutely
hopeless, and that even the blacks were better than we [the
mixed race] were, and he went back to this thing about their
hands being lighter, saying that it was like that because they
always went about with their hands folded together, praying in
secret.

I thought this was so funny, this thing of the blacks' hands
being lighter, that you should just see me now—I don't let go of
anybody, whoever they are, until they tell me why they think
that the palms of their hands are lighter. Dona Dores, for
instance told me that God made their hands lighter like that so
they wouldn't dirty the food they made for their masters, or
anything else they were ordered to do that should be kept quite
clean.

Senhor Antunes, the Coca-Cola man, who only comes to
the village now and again when all the cokes in the cantinas
have been sold, said to me that everything I had been told was a
lot of baloney. Of course I don't know if it was really, but he
assured me it was. After I said yes, all right, it was baloney, then
he told me what he knew about this thing of the blacks' hands.
It was like this: "Long ago, many years ago, God, our Lord
Jesus Christ, the Virgin Mary, St. Peter, many other saints, all
the angels that were in heaven then, and some of the people
who had died and gone to heaven—they all had a meeting and
decided to make blacks. Do you know how? They got hold of
some clay and pressed it into second-hand molds. And to bake
the clay of the creatures they took them to the heavenly kilns.
Because they were in a hurry and there was no room next to the
fire, they hung them in the chimneys. Smoke, smoke, smoke—
and there you have them, black as coals. And now do you want
to know why their hands stayed white? Well, didn't they have
to hold on while their clay baked?"

When he had told me this Senhor Antunas, and the other
men were around us all burst out laughing, they were so
pleased.

That very same day Senhor Firas called me after Senhor

Antunes had gone away and told me that everything I had heard from them had been just one big pack of lies. Really and truly, what he knew about the blacks was right—that God finished making men and told them to bathe in a lake in heaven. After bathing the people were nice and white. The blacks, well, they were made very early in the morning, and at this hour the water in the lake was very cold, so they only wet the palms of their hands and the soles of their feet before dressing and coming into the world.

But I read in a book that happened to mention it that the blacks have hands lighter like this because they spent all their days bent over, gathering the white cotton in Virginia and I don't know where else. Of course, Don Estefania didn't agree when I told her this. According to her, it's only because their hands became bleached with all the washing.

Well, I don't know what you'll think about all this, but the truth is that however callused and cracked they may be, a black's hands are always lighter than the rest of him. And that's that!

My mother is the only one who must be right about this question of a black's hands being lighter than the rest of his body. On the day that we were talking about this, we two, I was telling her what I already knew about the matter, and she couldn't stop laughing. What I found strange was that she didn't tell me at once what she thought about all this, and she only answered me when she was sure I wouldn't get tired of bothering her about it. And even then she was crying and clutching herself around the stomach as if she had laughed so much she couldn't bear it. What she said was more or less this:

"God made blacks because they had to be. They had to be, my son. He thought they really had to be . . . . . Afterward, He regretted having made them because the other men laughed at them and took them off to their homes and put them to serve as slaves or not much better. But because He couldn't make them all turn white, for those who were used to seeing them black would complain, He made it so that the palms of their hands would be exactly like the palms of other men's hands. And do you know why that was? Of course you don't know, and it's not surprising, because many, many people don't know. Well, listen: it was to show that what men do is only the work of men . . . that what men do is done by hands that are the same— hands of people who, if they had sense, would know that before everything else they are men. He must have been thinking of this when he made it so that the hands of the blacks would be the same as the hands of all those men who thank God they're not black."

After telling me this, my mother kissed my hands.

As I ran off into the yard to play ball, I thought to myself that I had never seen her cry so much when nobody had even hit her or anything.

Part I
The African Past

Introduction

African history may well be the oldest in the world. Archaeological discoveries in East, Central and Southern Africa indicate that humans have lived in sub-Saharan Africa for at least 4 million years, longer than anywhere else on earth. There is a good chance that the history of the human race—and therefore our common ancestry—can be traced to African origins.

Since the beginning, Africans have compiled a long list of accomplishments and made an impressive number of contributions to human history. The Western world, however, has not always recognized these contributions. For centuries, Africa was thought of as the "dark continent," a land of primitive people with little or no history worth studying. Today, we realize that the real "darkness" was in our own minds, in our ignorance of Africa. This recent awakening has taught us a number of facts about Africa that should give us cause for some humility:

—Centuries before the discovery of the "new world," Africa had thriving cities that were centers of trade and technology.

—As early as the 14th century Africa had centers of learning at Timbuktu and Jenne that drew scholars and theologians from throughout the Muslim world.

—During the Middle Ages, when justice throughout much of the world was determined by the sword, great kingdoms in Africa had courts of law.

—When the Normans invaded a little-known island called England in 1066 A.D., they could muster an army of only 15,000 soldiers. In the same year, the West African state of Ghana could put 200,000 warriors in the field.

—When the Arabs invaded Europe in the 8th century A.D., they were able to push all the way through Spain into France. When they invaded West Africa, they were stopped in their tracks.

—When most Europeans were still pagans, in the 4th century A.D., the ancient kingdom of Ethiopia (then called Aksum) was a center of Christianity and could claim to be the oldest Christian empire in the world; its stone churches, built in the 12th century, are among the wonders of the world.

These random facts illustrate only a small part of Africa's rich history. There are many more facts that might be mentioned, and still others that might not strike Westerners as significant but are nonetheless important. After all, Africans might consider the development of peaceful societies more significant than the development of great armies. They might consider the preservation of African religions more significant than the adoption of Christianity. In short, Africans might have their own idea of what constitutes an important history.

But no matter what standards we use, African history stands as an important pillar in the structure of human development. Why, then did the West fail to appreciate the significance of African history for so long? There are several reasons.

BIASED HISTORY

First, Western historians traditionally focused their attention on the history of states—such as ancient Egypt, Greece and Rome—and not on the history of other groupings of people, sometimes called stateless societies. From a Western point of view, states had the most sophisticated form of political organization; other social systems were considered inferior even if such systems served their people better than states did. While sub-Saharan Africa did produce large states, as we shall see, it was largely populated by smaller, more intimately organized groups. It was precisely these groups that Western historians overlooked.

Second, historians have tended to rely extensively, if not solely, on written records to reconstruct the past. Stateless societies produce few written records; hence, most African societies were deemed to have no history, *technically speaking.*

A third reason for the neglect of African history can be found in the slave trade, which Europeans, Americans and Arabs conducted from the 15th to the 19th century. To justify the capture and sale of Africans, Europeans and others had a need to think of Africans as inferior human beings, or not fully human at all. As a result they denied—consciously and unconsciously—that Africans had any culture or history.

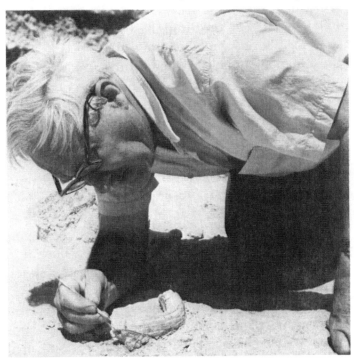

Dr. Louis Leakey, the late British archaeologist, was the first scholar to find evidence that clearly pointed to East Africa as the original home of human beings. Here he examines a piece of bone in Olduvai Gorge, in Tanzania. (Camerapix from Rapho Guillumette)

Fourth, when Europeans first established contact with Africa, they kept written records of what they saw and did; and although these records became important historical documents, in most cases they revealed the activities of Europeans, not of Africans. Consequently, our history of Africa has often been the history of Europeans *in* Africa.

Finally, when Europeans did write about Africans, they judged them according to their own (Western) standards. The result, of course, was a very slanted and negative interpretation of African life.

HISTORY REVISED

This neglect and distortion of African history has been reversed dramatically in recent years. Historians and other scholars have corrected many earlier biases and now recognize the high level of sophistication that many stateless societies achieved. Moreover, these changes in attitude have been accompanied by changes in methods of conducting research.

Historians have broadened their definition of what constitutes good historical evidence, reaching beyond the written word to other sources. In Africa, for example, most societies have well-developed systems of passing on information from one generation to the next by word of mouth. Historians have come to realize the importance of this *oral tradition* in learning about the African past. Today, it is possible to find historians scurrying around Africa, tape recorders in hand, interviewing village elders to capture the past before it is lost.

Modern archaeology and anthropology have also changed our view of the African past. People leave *things* behind, as well as words. Archaeologists can draw fairly detailed sketches of past cultures by examining the tools, art and architecture left behind. They can also determine the approximate age of such artifacts by using scientific dating techniques.

Scholars, then, have revised their interpretation of the African past by correcting earlier biases and by broadening their sources of information. Just as important, if not more so, the origin of the historians themselves has changed considera-

bly in recent years. Today, more and more African scholars are Africans and thus in a position to write their own histories from an inside point of view. Together, all these changes in the writing of African history have produced a larger, brighter, and more compelling picture of the African past.

Throughout this volume, we will try to look at African history through African eyes, whenever possible. Part I deals with a small slice of sub-Saharan African history prior to the coming of the European around the year 1450. It also explores the value of the oral tradition and of archaeology in reconstructing a people's history.

In a continent the size of Africa—the second largest after Asia, three times the size of the United States—there is not one history, but many. There are almost 1,000 ethnic groups in Africa, and each has a story to tell.

What follows is only a glimpse of a very long, complex history—a history the world is only now beginning to appreciate.

Ancient Ghana—Kingdom of Gold

❧ INTRODUCTION: Perhaps the most spectacular history in Africa comes from the Western Sudan, the area which today includes Mauritania, Mali, and Senegal.

For more than 600 years, from approximately 1000 to 1600 A.D., a series of powerful empires developed in the Sudan that compared favorably in size and wealth to any empire in the world at that time. They certainly exceeded the medieval states of Europe in these respects. This period has since become known as the "golden age" of West African history.

The Western Sudan consists of grasslands, or savannas, that mark the southernmost border of the Sahara Desert and the beginning of black Africa. Despite the desert, however, the people living there have a long tradition of trading with the Arabs of North Africa. As early as 400 B.C., Arab traders made the difficult journey across the desert to exchange their salt and cloth for Sudanese gold and ivory. In fact, it was the Arabs who gave the name "Sudan," meaning "black," to these grasslands of Africa. They called the area *Bilad as-Sudan*, the land of the blacks.

Early trade was hazardous and sometimes unprofitable because the horses and donkeys that carried the goods were ill-suited for desert travel. But around the year 100 A.D., the camel was imported from Asia. Not only did this animal have broad feet that did not sink into the sand, but it had the ability to store water and therefore could endure the long journeys between oases. Hundreds of camels could be gathered together to form long caravans. As a result, trade became more profitable and grew. It was not until the late seventh century, however, that the trade really flourished. At that time, the Muslims from the north invaded the Western Sudan, looking for converts to their religion as well as for increased trade.

This flurry of activity led to the formation of trading cities, which expanded into states and finally into empires. The first of

27

these empires of the Western Sudan was Ghana.

It is estimated that Ghana existed as early as 400 A.D. Certainly by the year 800 it was a thriving trading center, and by 1070 it was one of the most powerful empires in the world. "Ancient Ghana—Kingdom of Gold," deals with the high point of Ghana's development. It is based on documents of the time, as well as on evidence derived from archaeology and from the oral tradition.[2] ❧

The first time Ghana is mentioned in writing, in 772 A.D., it is called simply "the land of gold." In a sense, that brief description tells the whole story: namely, Ghana was very wealthy, and its wealth derived from gold.

A later writer, in the ninth century, went so far as to say that Ghana was "a country where gold grows like plants in the

Camel caravans are still used to transport goods across the Sahara Desert, employing the same elements of navigation as their ancestors: sun, stars, and wind patterns. Arab traders of North Africa made the dangerous trip to the Western Sudan as early as 400 B.C. Trade flourished after the introduction of the camel in A.D. 100.

sand in the same way as carrots do, and is plucked at sunset." Still another writer described the king of Ghana as "the wealthiest of all kings on the face of the earth on account of the riches he owns and the hoards of gold acquired by him and inherited from his predecessors since ancient time."

In fact, the king of Ghana was called "master of gold." However, he called himself "Ghana," meaning "warrior king." And since all the kings of Ghana prefaced their names with the title "Ghana," visitors mistakenly thought that this was the name of the state. The real name of the kingdom was Kumbi, and the people who lived there were called the Soninke. They spoke a language belonging to a family of languages that is still spoken by many West Africans.

The most complete account of ancient Ghana was written in 1067, at the height of Ghana's power, by the Arab scholar Al-Bakri. In describing the king's legal system, Al-Bakri gives us an idea of the empire's wealth as well as of its advanced political structure, complete with subordinate kings and governors.

> The court of appeal is held in a domed pavilion around which stand ten horses with gold embroidered trappings. Behind the king stand ten pages holding shields and swords decorated with gold, and on his right are the sons of the subordinate kings of his country, all wearing splendid garments and with their hair mixed with gold. The governor of the city sits on the ground before the king, and around him are ministers seated likewise. At the door of the pavilion are dogs of excellent pedigree which, guarding the king, hardly ever leave the place where he is. Round their necks they wear collars of gold and silver, studded with a number of balls of the same metals.

Another Arab writer claims that the king at this time had "a nugget of pure gold weighing thirty pounds, of absolutely natural formation," to which he tied his horse. Another writer several centuries later contends that a seventh-century king of Ghana had 1,000 horses, each one of which "slept only on a carpet, with a silken rope for halter." Moreover, each horse had three personal servants to take care of its needs.

WEALTH THROUGH TRADE

How did Ghana develop such wealth? The answer, as we have suggested, was by trading in gold. But, interestingly, Ghana never owned any goldfields of its own. It simply controlled the trade. The gold came from an area south of Ghana, called Wangara, which scholars place somewhere near

the Senegal River. The Wangara people, who are related to the
contemporary Fulani tribes of West Africa, never lost control of
their gold to Ghana, but they needed to trade their gold for salt
in order to survive. It might be said that the gold of Wangara
was worth its weight in salt.

The salt did not come from Ghana but from the Sahara
Desert and North Africa. The Arab traders of this region
wanted gold as much as the Wangara wanted salt, but both had
to pass through Ghana to trade. Ghana thus was in the perfect
position to serve as middleman. As long as it kept both sides
happy, it was able to control the trade.

The Wangara and the Arabs never came face to face in the
trade. Instead they conducted "dumb barter," or silent trade.
When the Arabs arrived in Ghana with their salt (as well as
other goods, such as silk, copper, and metal pots), they placed it
in piles along the river, with each trader marking his own pile
of goods for identification. They then beat drums to announce
the opening of the market.

The Wangara, upon hearing the drums, would sail up the
river with their gold and ivory. In the meantime, the Arabs

The glories of Ancient Ghana seem to be resurrected in this modern-day celebration in Kano, in northern Nigeria. (Leon E. Clark)

would retreat about a half day's journey away. When the Wangara arrived at the market, they would place their gold alongside each pile of goods, based on their estimation of its worth, and then withdraw.

If the Arabs were satisfied with the amount of gold left, they would sound the drums again, signaling the end of the barter. If they were not satisfied, they simply retreated once again and waited for the Wangara to increase their payment. This back-and-forth process continued until both sides were satisfied.

How was Ghana able to control this trade? What services

did it perform? After all, it produced neither the gold nor the salt. Why couldn't the Arabs and the Wangara conduct their own trade without Ghana?

One answer is power. Ghana controlled the land, as we have seen, but more important, it had the military forces to defeat its neighbors and absorb them into its empire, thereby gaining domination over the area. According to Al-Bakri, "When the king of Ghana calls up his army, he can put 200,000 men in the field, more than 40,000 of whom are bowmen." This was undoubtedly one of the largest armies in the world at the time.

Moreover, Ghana did provide services that allowed it to control the trade. First, because of the size of its army, it could maintain peace in the area, thereby assuring safe trade for the Arabs and the Wangara. Second, it maintained the value of the gold by limiting the amount that was traded. Al-Bakri writes, "The nuggets found in all the mines of this country are reserved for the king, only gold dust being left for the people. Without this precaution, the people would accumulate gold until it had lost its value." Ghana, then, stabilized the trade by holding a monopoly over the gold. Again, it could do this because of its power.

But how did Ghana develop its power initially? After all, before it could afford its huge army, it had to have wealth, and before it developed its wealth, it had to have control over the territory through which the traders passed. How did it manage to defeat its neighbors?

FACTORS OF STRENGTH

There is no simple answer to this question. There are always many factors that lead to the domination of one state over another. In the case of Ghana, however, there are at least three or four factors that we can point to with assurance.

First, Ghana had superior technology. It had developed the art of iron work to the point where it could make spears. These weapons clearly gave Ghana an advantage in the field. Second, Ghana had excellent organization. At the top of the social system was the king. But under him, as we have seen, were subordinate kings and governors who ruled throughout the empire. They paid their final allegiance (as well as money) to the king, however, for in return they received protection and the right to rule their local areas.

An illustration of Ghana's excellent organization can be found in its tax system, an advanced social technique at the time. Al-Bakri writes: "For every donkey loaded with salt that enters the country, the king takes a duty of one golden *dinar* [⅛ oz. of gold] and two *dinars* from every one that leaves. From a load of copper the duty due to the king is five *mitqals* [worth one fifth of a *dinar*], and from a load of merchandise ten *mitqals*."

Another form of taxation involved food. The peasants living outside the trading centers contributed a certain amount of their production each year to the cities, thereby freeing the traders and craftsmen to do other work. Ghana's ability to feed its own people was another key factor in its rise to power.

A fourth factor, closely related to social organization, was that Ghana had strong and wise leadership. The king, although he had a council of advisors, made all the important decisions himself. Moreover, he used his strength to ensure justice throughout the empire; he personally held court and judged cases. At the same time, the king could be diplomatic. For example, he invited the Muslim traders of the north to come to Ghana to live and allowed them to set up a town six miles away from his capital, in Kumbi. As long as the Muslims paid their taxes, they were welcome in Ghana.

Al-Bakri describes this agreement:

The city of Ghana [Khumbi—with a population of 15,000] consists of two towns lying in a plain. One of these towns is inhabited by Muslims. It is large and possesses twelve mosques [Muslim houses of worship]. There are *Imams* and *muezzins* [religious leaders] and assistants as well as jurists and learned men. Around the town are wells of sweet water from which they drink and near which they grow vegetables. The town in which the king lives is six miles from the Muslim one. The land

*Empires have risen and fallen on their ability to find supplies of salt, a scarce
commodity in many parts of Africa. This picture shows slabs of solid salt, formed by
filling small pools with spring water which soaks up salt from the desert and then
evaporates. (Afrique Photo, Cliche Naud, Paris)*

between the two towns is covered with houses. The houses of
the inhabitants are made of stone and acacia wood. The king
has a palace and a number of dome-shaped dwellings, the
whole surrounded by an enclosure like the defensive wall of a
city. In the town where the king lives, and not far from the hall
where he holds his court of justice, is a mosque where the
Muslims pray when visiting on diplomatic missions.

The king of Ghana himself and most of his people
followed their own traditional African religion. Their common belief was perhaps another factor making Ghana strong
and unified. And certainly the king's ability to integrate
different religions in his kingdom led to cooperation.

Ancient Ghana, then, was an extremely complex empire.

It possessed many of the characteristics of powerful nations today: wealth based on trade, sufficient food to feed its people, income derived from taxes, social organization that ensured justice and efficient political control, a strong army equipped with advanced weapons, and a foreign policy that led to peace and cooperation with other people.

Such advanced development is no small accomplishment for any nation at any time. Ghana was able to achieve it more than 1,000 years ago.

POSTSCRIPT: The present-day nation of Ghana won its independence in 1957. A year earlier, when Ghana was still called the Gold Coast, Kwame Nkrumah, independence leader and Ghana's first president, made the following comments in a speech to the Gold Coast Assembly.[3]

The Government proposes that when the Gold Coast attains independence, the name of the country should be changed from "Gold Coast" to the new name of "Ghana." The name Ghana is rooted deeply in ancient African history, especially in the history of the western portion of Africa known as the Western Sudan. It kindles in the imagination of modern African youth the grandeur and the achievements of a great medieval civilization which our ancestors developed many centuries before European penetration and subsequent domination of Africa began . . .

For the one thousand years that the Ghana Empire existed, it spread over . . . the greater part of West Africa— namely, from Nigeria in the east to Senegambia in the west. While it existed, the Ghana Empire carried on extensive commercial relations with the outside world—extending as far as Spain and Portugal . . . It is reported that Egyptian, European, and Asiatic students attended the great and famous universities and other institutions of higher learning that flourished in Ghana during the medieval period to learn philosophy, mathematics, medicine, and law.

It is from this rich historical background that the name Ghana has been proposed as the new name of the Gold Coast

upon the attainment of independence; we take pride in the
name, not out of romanticism, but as an inspiration for the
future.

The Kingdom of Mali

✣ INTRODUCTION: As we have seen, Ghana was the first of the great West African kingdoms because of its development and control of the trans-Saharan trade in gold. But like all empires, it did not last forever. In the eleventh century, the Muslims from the north made repeated attacks on Ghana. They never succeeded in subjugating the empire, but they weakened it enough to make way for the second of the great Sudanic states, Mali.

The empire of Mali had existed as early as the year 1000, and when Ghana fell apart 100 years later, it was able to form a new and powerful state. Using the same methods as Ghana for controlling trade and administering its territory, Mali went on to become even more wealthy and powerful than its predecessor.

The man most responsible for Mali's rise to greatness was Sundiata Keita, who ruled from 1230 to 1255. He not only succeeded in capturing the gold fields of Wangara but expanded the old Ghana empire to include large stretches of the Sahara to the north and east, as well as parts of present-day Guinea and Senegal, to the south and west.

We will learn more about Sundiata in the next selection. Here we will learn of a later king of Mali, Mansa Musa, who followed Sundiata by almost sixty years (he was in fact Sundiata's grand-nephew) and became even more powerful and famous than Sundiata.

Mansa Musa ascended the throne in 1312 and immediately established himself as an excellent administrator. Building on the foundations laid by Sundiata, he expanded the empire even further, absorbing the trading centers of Timbuktu and Gao. He also united the various chiefs in the empire under his strong rule. The result was that by the time of Musa's death, in 1337, Mali had become one of the largest empires in the world and by far the richest that Africa has ever known.

37

The selection that follows describes Mansa Musa's pilgrimage to Mecca in 1324. By this time, most of the leaders in the Western Sudan, and many of the people, were Muslim. It is traditional for all Muslims to make a pilgrimage to Mecca at least once in their lifetime, if at all possible. During his trip, Mansa Musa dazzled the city of Cairo with his wealth, much of which he gave away to charity. It is said that Mansa Musa's caravan consisted of 60,000 people and 100 camels, each carrying 300 pounds of gold dust.

The rest of this selection deals with the size of Mansa Musa's empire and the nature of his rule. You will notice that the Muslim religion, which Musa followed devoutly, plays an important role in the legal system of Mali.

The entire selection consists of five parts: the first three were written by Ibn Fadl Allah al Omari; the last two, by Ibn Battuta. Both writers were important Arab scholars of the fourteenth century. Al Omari visited Cairo only twelve years after Mansa Musa's famous visit. Ibn Battuta visited Mali personally. Indeed, Ibn Battuta, a Berber born in Morocco in 1304, is considered by many to be "the

greatest and most inexhaustible traveler in the history of the world, "
having covered more than 73,000 miles in what are now 44 countries,
all without motorized transportation. [4] ❧

MANSA MUSA GOES TO CAIRO

During my first journey to Cairo and sojourn there I heard
talk of the arrival of the Sultan Musa [Mansa Musa, emperor of
Mali] and I found the Cairenes [residents of Cairo] very glad to
talk of the large expenditures of those people.

I questioned the Emir [the Muslim leader], who spoke of
the sultan's noble appearance, dignity, and trustworthiness.
"When I went out to greet him in the name of the glorious
Sultan el Malik en Nasir [of Egypt]," he told me, "he gave me
the warmest of welcomes and treated me with the most careful
politeness. But he would talk to me only through an interpreter [that is, his spokesman or linguist] although he could speak
perfect Arabic. He carried his imperial treasure in many pieces
of gold, worked or otherwise.

"I suggested that he [Mansa Musa] should go up to the
palace and meet the Sultan [of Egypt]. But he refused, saying: 'I
came for the pilgrimage, and for nothing else, and I do not
wish to mix up my pilgrimage with anything else.' He argued
about this. However, I well understood that the meeting was
repugnant to him because he was loath to kiss the ground
[before the Sultan] or to kiss his hand. I went on insisting and
he went on making excuses. But imperial protocol obliged me
to present him and I did not leave him until he had agreed.

"When he came into the Sultan's presence we asked him to
kiss the ground. But he refused and continued to refuse, saying:
'However can this be?' Then a wise man of his suite whispered
several words to him that I could not understand. 'Very well,'
he thereupon declared, 'I will prostrate myself before Allah
who created me and brought me into the world.' Having done
so he moved toward the Sultan. The latter rose for a moment to
welcome him and asked him to sit beside him: then they had a
long conversation. After Sultan Musa had left the palace the
Sultan of Cairo sent him gifts of clothing for himself, his

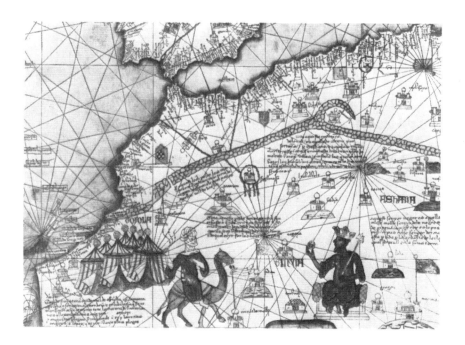

Mansa Musa, king of Ancient Mali, holds a huge gold nugget in his hand, attracting an Arab trader. This map, drawn in 1375, comes from Catalan, Spain. The extent of the Mali empire is shown by the defensive wall arching across the Sahara Desert in the upper part of the picture. (Courtesy of the Trustees of the British Museum)

courtiers, and all those who were with him; saddled and bridled horses for himself and his chief officers . . .

"When the time of pilgrimage arrived, [the Sultan of Egypt] sent him a large quantity of drachmas [Egyptian coins], baggage camels, and choice riding-camels with saddles and harness. [The Sultan of Egypt] caused abundant quantities of foodstuffs to be bought for [Musa's] suite and his followers, established posting-stations for the feeding of the animals, and gave to the emirs of the pilgrimage a written order to look after and respect [the Emperor of Mali]. When the latter returned, it was I who went to greet him and settle him into this quarters . . . .

"This man," el Mehmendar also told me, "spread upon Cairo the flood of his generosity: there was no person, officer of the court, or holder of any office of the [Cairo] sultanate who did not receive a sum in gold from him. The people of Cairo earned incalculable sums from him, whether by buying and selling or by gifts. So much gold was current in Cairo that it ruined the value of money . . . ."

Let me add that gold in Egypt had enjoyed a high rate of exchange up to the moment of their arrival. The gold *mitqal* that year had not fallen below twenty-five drachmas. But from that day [of Musa's arrival] onward, its value dwindled; the exchange was ruined, and even now it has not recovered. The *mitqal* scarcely touches twenty-two drachmas. That is how it has been for twelve years from that time, because of the great amounts of gold they brought to Egypt and spent there.

THE EXTENT OF THE MALI EMPIRE

The king of this country is known to the people of Egypt as the king of Tekrur; but he himself becomes indignant when he is called thus, since Tekrur is only one of the countries of his empire [roughly, inland Senegal]. The title he prefers is . . . lord of Mali, the largest of his states; it is the name by which he is most known. He is the most important of the Muslim Negro kings; his land is the largest, his army the most numerous; he is the king who is the most powerful, the richest, the most fortunate, the most feared by his enemies, and the most able to do good to those around him . . . .

The honorable and truthful Sheikh Abu Sa'id Otman ed Dukkali, who has lived in the town of Niane for thirty-five years and traveled throughout the kingdom, has told me that this is square in shape, being four months [of travel] in length and at least as much in breadth . . . .

The sultan of this country has sway over the land of the "desert of gold," whence they bring him gold every year. The inhabitants of that land are savage pagans whom the sultan would subject to him if he wished. But the sovereigns of this kingdom have learned by experience that whenever one of them has conquered one of these gold towns, established Islam there, and sounded the call to prayer, the harvest of gold dwindles and falls to nothing; meanwhile it grows and expands in neighboring pagan countries. When experience had confirmed them in this observation, they left the gold country in the hands of its pagan inhabitants and contented themselves with assuring their obedience and paying tribute.

THE COURT

The sultan of this kingdom presides in his palace on a great balcony, called *bembe*, where he has a great seat of ebony that is like a throne fit for a large and tall person: on either side it is flanked by elephant tusks turned toward each other. His arms stand near him, being all of gold—saber, lance, quiver, bow, and arrows. He wears wide trousers made of about twenty pieces [of cloth], of a kind which he alone may wear.

Behind him there stand about a score of Turkish or other pages which are bought for him in Cairo: one of them, at his left, holds a silk umbrella surmounted by a dome and a bird of gold: the bird has the figure of a falcon. His officers are seated in a circle about him, in two rows, one to the right and one to the left; beyond them sit the chief commanders of his cavalry.

In front of him there is a person who never leaves him and who is his executioner; also another who serves as intermediary [that is, official spokesman] between the sovereign and his subjects, and who is named the herald. In front of them, again, there are drummers. Others dance before their sovereign, who enjoys this, and make him laugh. Two banners are spread behind him. Before him they keep two saddled and bridled horses in case he should wish to ride.

Arab horses are brought for sale to the kings of this country, who spend considerable sums in this way. Their army numbers 100,000 men of whom there are about 10,000 horse-mounted cavalry: the others are infantry having neither horses nor any other mounts. They have camels in this country but do not know the art of riding them with a saddle. . . .

The officers of this king, his soldiers, and his guard receive gifts of land and presents. Some among the greatest of them receive as much as 50,000 *mitqals* of gold a year, besides which the king provides them with horses and clothing. He is much

The city of Jenne, one of the major trading centers of Ancient Mali, exhibits the architectural styles typical of the Western Sudan. The buildings are constructed of clay, made from the sand of the Sahara. The ornate structure shown below is a mosque. (Afrique Photo, Cliche Naud, Paris)

concerned with giving them fine garments and making his cities into capitals.

POMP AND CIRCUMSTANCE

On certain days the sultan holds audiences in the palace yard, where there is a platform under a tree, with three steps; this they call the *pempi*. It is carpeted with silk and has cushions placed on it. [Over it] is raised the umbrella which is a sort of pavilion made of silk, surmounted by a bird in gold, about the size of a falcon.

The sultan comes out of a door in a corner of the palace, carrying a bow in his hand and a quiver on his back. On his head he has a golden skullcap, bound with a gold band which has narrow ends shaped like knives, more than a span in length. His usual dress is a velvety red tunic, made of the European fabric called *mutanfas*. The sultan is preceded by his musicians, who carry gold and silver *guimbris* [two-stringed guitars], and behind him come three hundred armed slaves.

He walks in a leisurely fashion, affecting a very slow movement, and even stops from time to time. On reaching the *pempi* he stops and looks round the assembly, then ascends it in the sedate manner of a preacher ascending a mosque-pulpit. As he takes his seat the drums, trumpets, and bugles are sounded. Three slaves go out at a run to summon the sovereign's deputy and the military commanders, who enter and sit down. Two saddled and bridled horses are brought, along with two goats, which they hold to serve as a protection against the evil eye. Dugha [musician] stands at the gate and the rest of the people remain in the street, under the trees.

The Negroes are of all people the most submissive to their king and the most abject in their behavior before him. They swear by his name. . . . If he summons any of them while he is holding an audience in his pavilion, the person summoned takes off his clothes and puts on warm garments, removes his turban, and dons a dirty skullcap, and enters with his garments and trousers raised knee-high. He goes forward in an attitude of humility and dejection, knocks the ground hard with his elbows, then stands with bowed head and bent back listening to what [the sultan] says.

If anyone addresses the king and receives a reply from him, [that person] uncovers his back and throws dust over his head and back, for all the world like a bather splashing himself with water. I used to wonder how it was they did not blind themselves. If the sultan delivers any remarks during his audience, those present take off their turbans and put them down, and listen in silence to what he says.

Sometimes one of them stands up before him and recalls his deeds in the sultan's service, saying "I did so-and-so on such a day" or "I killed so-and-so on such a day." Those who have knowledge of this confirm his words, which they do by plucking the cord of the bow and releasing it [with a twang], just as an archer does when shooting an arrow. If the sultan says "truly spoken" or thanks him, [the man] removes his clothes and "dusts." That is their idea of good manners.

SECURITY AND JUSTICE

Among the admirable qualities of these people, the following are to be noted:

1. The small number of acts of injustice that one finds there; for the Negroes are of all peoples those who most abhor injustice. The sultan pardons no one who is guilty of it.

2. The complete and general safety one enjoys throughout the land. The traveler has no more reason than the man who stays at home to fear brigands, thieves, or ravishers.

3. The blacks do not confiscate the goods of white men (that is, North Africans) who die in their country, not even when these consist of big treasures. They deposit them, on the contrary, with a man of confidence among the whites until those who have a right to the goods present themselves and take possession.

4. They make their prayers punctually; they assiduously attend their meetings of the faithful, and punish their children if they should fail in this. On Fridays, anyone who is late at the mosque will find nowhere to pray, the crowd is so great. Their

custom is to send their servants to the mosque to spread their prayer-mats in the due and proper place, and to remain there until they, the masters, should arrive. . . .

5. The Negroes wear fine white garments on Fridays. If by chance a man has no more than one shirt . . . at least he washes it before putting it on to go to public prayer.

6. They zealously learn the Koran [the Muslim holy book] by heart. Those children who are neglectful in this are put in chains until they have memorized the Koran. On one festival day I visited the *qadi* and saw children thus enchained and asked him: "Will you not let them free?" He replied: "Only when they know their Koran by heart."

Another day I was passing by a young Negro, a handsome lad and very well dressed, who had a heavy chain on his feet. I said to my companion: "What's happened to the boy? Has he murdered someone?" The young Negro heard what I had said and began laughing. "They have chained him," I was told, "simply to make him memorize the Koran."

Griots: The Oral Tradition

✍ INTRODUCTION: Much of our information about Mali comes from the oral tradition. Indeed, much of our information about the early history of every part of the world comes to us through legends that were transmitted orally. But the oral history of West Africa is particularly important because of a remarkable group of people called *griots* (pronounced *gree-oes*).

The griots are professional historians, specially trained through years of study to remember all the important facts about their people, which they hand down from generation to generation. They are also poets and musicians—a type of troubadour. But they are more than this. Traditionally, griots have been assigned to important families, most notably to kings, whom they serve as advisors, masters of ceremonies, and official spokesmen. In the last selection, both the herald for Mansa Musa and the musician were griots.

For many centuries, then, the griots have been close to the seats of power. They have served as intermediaries between the rulers and the people. As court historians, they have also had the responsibility of reminding kings of the traditions they must uphold. The kings listened because the griots knew of what they spoke; today historians are beginning to listen too.

Alex Haley, the American writer and author of *Roots*, discovered his place of origin in West Africa by listening to the recitation of a griot, telling of events that happened hundreds of years ago.

In this selection you will meet a living griot, from Guinea. His name is Djeli Mamoudou Kouyate, and for centuries his family has served the Keita princes of Mali, including Sundiata Keita, the first great ruler of ancient Mali.[5] ✍

I am a griot. It is I, Djeli Mamoudou Kouyate, son of Bintou Kouyate and Djeli Kedian Kouyate, master in the art of

47

eloquence. Since time immemorial the Kouyates have been in the service of the Keita princes of Mali; we are vessels of speech, we are the repositories which harbor secrets many centuries old. The art of eloquence has no secrets for us; without us the names of kings would vanish into oblivion, we are the memory of mankind; by the spoken word we bring to life the deeds and exploits of kings for younger generations.

I derive my knowledge from my father, Djeli Kedian, who also got it from his father; history holds no mystery for us; we teach to the vulgar just as much as we want to teach them, for it is we who keep the keys to the twelve doors of Mali [i.e., the twelve provinces of which Mali was originally composed].

I know the list of all the sovereigns who succeeded to the throne of Mali. I know how the black people divided into tribes, for my father bequeathed to me all his learning; I know why such and such is called Kamara, another Keita, and yet another Sibibe or Traore; every name has a meaning, a secret import.

I teach kings the history of their ancestors so that the lives of the ancients might serve them as an example, for the world is old, but the future springs from the past.

My word is pure and free of all untruth; it is the word of my father; it is the word of my father's father. I will give you my father's words just as I received them; royal griots do not know what lying is. When a quarrel breaks out between tribes it is we who settle the difference, for we are the depositaries of oaths which the ancestors swore.

Listen to my word, you who want to know; by my mouth you will learn the history of Mali. By my mouth you will get to know the story of the ancestor of great Mali, the story of him who, by his exploits, surpassed even Alexander the Great; he who, from the East, shed his rays upon all the countries of the West.

Listen to the story of the son of the Buffalo, the son of the Lion. I am going to tell you of Maghan Sundiata, of Mari Djata, of Sogolon Djata, or Nare Maghan Djata; the man of many names against whom sorcery could avail nothing.

THE FIRST KINGS OF MALI

Listen, then, sons of Mali, children of the black people, listen to my word, for I am going to tell you of Sundiata, the father of the Bright Country, of the savanna land, the ancestor of those who draw the bow, the master of a hundred vanquished kings. I am going to talk of Sundiata, Manding Diara, Lion of Mali, Sogolon Djata, son of Sogolon, Nare Maghan Djata, son of Nare Maghan, Sogo Sogo Simbon Salaba, hero of many names. I am going to tell you of Sundiata, he whose exploits will astonish men for a long time yet. He was great among kings; he was peerless among men; he was beloved of God because he was the last of the great conquerors.

Right at the beginning, then, Mali, was a province of the Bambara kings; those who are today called Mandingo, inhabitants of Mali, are not indigenous [local]; they come from the East. Bilali Bounama, ancestor of the Keitas, was the faithful servant of the prophet Muhammad (may the peace of God be upon him). Bilali Bounama had seven sons of whom the eldest, Lawalo, left the Holy City and came to settle in Mali; Lawalo had Latal Kalabi for a son, Latal Kalabi had Damul Kalabi, who then had Lahilatoul Kalabi.

Lahilatoul Kalabi was the first black prince to make the pilgrimage to Mecca. On his return he was robbed by brigands in the desert; his men were scattered and some died of thirst, but God saved Lahilatoul Kalabi, for he was a righteous man. He called upon the Almighty, and jinn [the spirit] appeared and recognized him as king. After seven years' absence Lahilatoul was able to return, by the grace of Allah the Almighty, to Mali, where none expected to see him any more.

Lahilatoul Kalabi had two sons, the elder being called Kalabi Bomba and the younger Kalabi Dauman; the elder chose royal power and reigned, while the younger preferred fortune and wealth and became the ancestor of those who go from country to country seeking their fortune.

Kalabi Bomba had Mamadi Kani for a son. Mamadi Kani was a hunter king like the first kings of Mali; . . . he communicated with the jinn of the forest and bush. These

A young historian from the Ivory Coast tapes the ancient legends of the Akan people,
as told by one of the chiefs. Notice the drum accompaniment in the background.
(Marc and Evelyne Bernheim from Rapho Guillumette)

spirits had no secrets from him, and he was loved by Kondolon Ni Sane [gods of the chase]. His followers were so numerous that he formed them into an army which became formidable; he often gathered them together in the bush and taught them the art of hunting. It was he who revealed to hunters the medicinal leaves which heal wounds and cure diseases. Thanks to the strength of his followers, he became king of a vast country; with them Mamadi Kani conquered all the lands which stretch from the Sankarani to the Boure. Mamadi Kani had four sons—Kani Simbon, Kamignogo Simbon, Kabala Simbon, and Simbon Tagnogokelin. They were all initiated into the art of hunting and deserved the title of Simbon [great hunter]. It was the lineage of Bamari Tagnogokelin which held on to the power; his son was M'Bali Nene, whose son was Bello. Bello's son was called Bello Bakon, and he had a son called Maghan Kon Fatta, also called Frako Maghan Keigu, Maghan the handsome.

Maghan Kon Fatta was the father of the great Sundiata and had three wives and six children—three boys and three girls. His first wife was called Sassouma Berete, daughter of a great divine; she was the mother of King Dankaran Touman and Princess Nana Triban. The second wife, Sogolon Kedjou, was the mother of Sundiata and the two princesses Sogolon Kolonkan and Sogolon Djamarou. The third wife was one of the Kamaras and was called Namandje; she was the mother of Manding Bory (or Manding Bakary), who was the best friend of his half-brother Sundiata. . . .

ETERNAL MALI

Mali keeps its secrets jealously. There are things which the uninitiated will never know, for the griots, their depositaries, will never betray them. Maghan Sundiata, the last conqueror on earth, lies not far from Niani-Niani at Balandougou. . . .

After him many kings and many Mansas [sultans] reigned over Mali, and other towns sprang up and disappeared. Hajji Mansa Moussa [Musa], of illustrious memory, beloved of God, built houses at Mecca for pilgrims coming from Mali, but the towns which he founded have all disappeared. Karaniana, Bouroun-Kouna—nothing more remains of these towns. Other kings carried Mali far beyond Djata's frontiers—for example, Mansa Samanka and Fadima Moussa—but none of them came near Djata.

Maghan Sundiata was unique. In his own time no one equalled him, and after him no one had the ambition to surpass him. He left his mark on Mali, for all time, and his taboos still guide men in their conduct.

Mali is eternal. To convince yourself of what I have said go to Mali. At Tigan you will find the forest dear to Sundiata. There you see Fakoli Koroma's plastron [medieval breast-plate]. Go to Kirikoroni near Niassola and you will see a tree which commemorates Sundiata's passing through these parts. Go to Bankoumana on the Niger and you will see Soumaoro's balafon [xylophone-like musical instrument]. Go to Ka-ba and you will see the clearing of Kouroukan Fougan, where the great assembly took place which gave Sundiata's empire its constitution. Go to Krina near Ka-ba and you will see the bird that foretold the end to Soumaoro. At Keyla, near Ka-ba, you will find the royal drums belonging to Djolofin Mansa, king of Senegal, whom Djata defeated. But never try, wretch, to pierce the mystery which Mali hides from you. Do not go and disturb the spirits in their eternal rest. Do not ever go into the dead cities to question the past, for the spirits never forgive. Do not seek to know what is not to be known.

Men of today, how small you are beside your ancestors, and small in mind too, for you have trouble in grasping the meaning of my words. Sundiata rests near Niani-Niani, but his spirit lives on, and today the Keitas still come and bow before the stone under which lies the father of Mali.

To acquire my knowledge I have journeyed all round Mali. At Kita I saw the mountain where the lake of holy water sleeps; at Segou I learned the history of the kings of Do and Kri; at Fadama, in Hamana, I heard the Konde griots relate how the Keitas, Kondes, and Kamaras conquered Wouroula. At Keyla, the village of the great masters, I learned the origins of Mali and the art of speaking. Everywhere I was able to see and understand what my masters were teaching me, but between their hands I took an oath to teach only what is to be taught and to conceal what is to be kept concealed.

Sun, Science, and History

❧ INTRODUCTION: The oral tradition in Africa is not always preserved by "professionals," such as griots. Sometimes it is simply the responsibility of the elders to pass on their knowledge to the younger generation. In either case, the responsibility is taken very seriously.

The information, however, no matter how accurate it is, refers to only one family or group of people. How do we know the dates of these events? The following selection illustrates one way in which the oral tradition can be dated.[6] ❧

Some fifty years ago, in a clearing of the Congo forest, a Hungarian in Belgian service sat making notes. For the time and place this Hungarian, Emil Torday, was an unusual sort of man, an unusual sort of European. What he wanted was neither rubber nor ivory nor conscript labor, but information about the past.

And he had come far in search of it. After traveling for many hundred miles up the Congo River from its Atlantic mouth he had continued on his way into the heart of Africa. He had traveled up the Kasai River and then along the banks of the Sankuru, and now, somewhere in the dense green middle of an Africa that was almost completely unknown to the outside world, he had reached the Bushongo people, and sat listening to their chiefs and making notes.

For the benefit of this European, one of the first they had ever set eyes on, the elders of the Bushongo recalled the legends and tradition of their past. That was not in the least difficult for them, since remembering the past was one of their duties. They unrolled their story in measured phrases. They went on

These giant walls, measuring 32 feet high and 17 feet thick and consisting of 900,000 large granite blocks, form part of the ruins of Great Zimbabwe, a southern African kingdom that flourished for several hundred years beginning in about 1000 A.D. It is located in the center of modern-day Zimbabwe, which derives its name from this medieval kingdom. "Zimbabwe" means stone houses in the Shona language.

Europeans first became aware of Great Zimbabwe in 1868 when a European hunter stumbled upon the ruins. At the time, and until very recently, many Europeans thought the ruins were left by white men who had passed through the area. Europeans were reluctant to give credit to Africans for such an impressive achievement. Not only did the ruins indicate an advanced civilization, but they displayed a building technique found nowhere else in Africa. (Notice the skillful way in which the stones are placed one on top of another.) Moreover, gold objects were found (and looted by Europeans), which led some Europeans to speculate that Great Zimbabwe was the site of the legendary King Solomon's mines.

However, when archaeologists investigated Great Zimbabwe in 1905 and again in 1929, they found "not one single item that was not in accordance with the claim of Bantu origin and medieval date." Zimbabwe was indeed the political and religious center of a large empire that survived for more than 400 years, deriving much of its wealth from local gold deposits. Because of a shortage of salt, the inhabitants had moved north by the time the Europeans arrived, in the 16th century.

The case of Great Zimbabwe is an excellent example of how archaeology can help to solve the "mysteries" of African history. (FPG) and on. They were not to be hurried. They traversed the list of the kings, a list of one hundred and twenty names, right back to the god-king whose marvels had founded their nation.

It was splendid, but was it history? Could any of these kings be given a date, be linked—at least in time—to the history of the rest of the world? Torday was an enthusiast and went on making notes, but he longed for a date. And quite suddenly they gave it to him.

"As the elders were talking of the great events of various reigns," he remembered afterwards, "and we came to the ninety-eighth chief, Bo Kama Bomanchala, they said that nothing remarkable had happened during his reign, except that one day at noon the sun went out, and there was absolute darkness for a short time.

"When I heard this I lost all self-control. I jumped up and wanted to do something desperate. The elders thought that I had been stung by a scorpion.

"It was only months later that the date of the eclipse became known to me . . . the thirtieth of March, 1680, when there was a total eclipse of the sun, passing exactly over Bushongo . . .

"There was no possibility of confusion with another eclipse, because this was the only one visible in the region during the seventeenth and eighteenth centuries."

The Rise of Songhay

✷ INTRODUCTION: The third and last of the great early empires of the Western Sudan was Songhay. It existed as early as the 9th century, but it did not rise to great power until the decline of Mali, in the 15th century.

After Mansa Musa's death in 1332, Mali began to lose control of its empire. First the important trading centers of Gao and Timbuktu reasserted their independence from Mali, which they had lost to Mansa Musa in 1325, and then eventually the whole empire collapsed. Mali's long fall from greatness, however, took almost 150 years.

The three empires ruled in approximately these periods: Ghana, 900-1067 A.D.; Mali, 1240-1332; Songhay, 1464-1528. The years in between are periods in which the declining empire had not yet lost all its former power and the new empire had not yet gained complete control.

The first section of this reading describes the capture of Timbuktu in 1468 by Sunni Ali Ber, the founder of the Songhay empire. Sunni Ali ascended the throne of Sonhay in 1464, and until his death in 1492 he never lost a battle. He is still a great hero in West Africa.

The second section of the reading deals with the reign of Askia Muhammad, or Askia the Great, as he is often called, who ruled from 1493 to 1528. During this period he greatly expanded the Songhay empire, making it eventually the largest of the three kingdoms, about two-thirds the size of the United States.[7] ✷

The chain of conquests which forged a great Songhay Empire began with the capture of Timbuktu around the year 1468. Perhaps the word "recapture" should be used. Timbuktu was probably founded by the people of the Niger, and it was traditionally regarded as a Songhay city. On the Great Bend of the Niger River, it was a place where the people of the river came to trade with the nomads of the desert.

During the years of the Empire of Mali, Timbuktu was already a center of commerce and one of the major centers of learning in all of Africa. It is no wonder that it was a prized possession of Mali. It had a great university, Sankore, which attracted many students from distant parts of Africa. Scholarship and commerce were the glories of Timbuktu.

Timbuktu was a crowded and fairly drab-looking town. Except for a mosque and a palace (built for Mansa Musa by Es-Saheli, the poet-architect), the town was said to be little more than "a mass of ill-looking houses, built of mud-bricks."

Mali's hold on Timbuktu weakened after the death of Mansa Musa. Around 1433 the city was invaded by Tuareg nomads from the desert. Their leader was a chief named Akil.

Though Timbuktu was his, Chief Akil chose not to live there. Instead he remained in the desert and appointed a man named Ammar to represent him in Timbuktu. One of Ammar's duties was to collect taxes. He kept one-third of the money himself and turned two-thirds over to Chief Akil.

When Ammar heard of the growing strength of the Sunni rulers of Songhay, he unwisely sent a letter to Sunni Ali Ber in Gao and boasted that Timbuktu could repulse any attack. Later he was sorry about this letter.

. . .Sunni Ali Ber was not going to let an opportunity like this slip by. He ordered his army to march at once on Timbuktu. Sunni Ali Ber himself rode at the head of his cavalry.

The Songhay army moved along the bank of the Niger. When they reached a city which was a "suburb" of Timbuktu, they were seen by Chief Alik and Ammar, who were watching from a hilltop.

The sight of the huge army from Songhay so unnerved

Akil that he decided to flee. Many of the Sankore teachers also
left as soon as they could. The Sankore scholars had loudly
scorned the people of Songhay as something on the level of
uncouth savages. Now that the Songhay army was on Timbuktu's shores, the timid scholars were not going to test the anger
of the people whom they had insulted. . . .

The Songhay army plundered Timbuktu and slew hundreds of its citizens. Sunni Ali was especially cruel to those
accused of having traded with the Tuaregs. For Sunni Ali
considered the Tuaregs his bitterest enemies. This was the
result of decades of Tuareg-Songhay rivalry for control of the
Middle Niger.

In a famous history of the Sudan, the historian Es-Sadi
described Sunni Ali as a "master tyrant" and "scoundrel." Like
many other Moslem writers, Es-Sadi could never forgive Sunni
Ali for his cruel and humiliating treatment of the Moslem
scholars of Timbuktu, especially since the Songhay king was
supposed to be a Moslem himself. Almost without exception,
Moslem historians tended to heap scorn on Sunni Ali.

Yet there was no doubt that Sunni Ali was revered by his
own people. They called him "the most high," implying that
he was like a god. His ability on the battlefield humbled those
who stood against him. Because he was headstrong, he was
often unpredictable. If he was cruel, he was also generous.
Above all else, Sunni Ali was an able ruler with a real talent for
organization and government.

THE NEW DYNASTY

. . . Askia Muhammad is remembered for his great achievements in unifying a huge area of land. Whereas the empire of
Sunni Ali Ber remained largely a confederation of individual
states, all paying allegiance to the Songhay emperor, the Askia
took central government in the western Sudan yet another
step.

He appointed governors to each of his provinces. In
addition he organized a central government of ministers
directly responsible to the king. This ministry included a

treasurer, the chief of the navy (of the Songhay canoe fleet), chief tax collector, and chiefs of forests, woodcutters, and fishermen. Each town or large village was governed by a person appointed by the king.

To strengthen the Moslem faith throughout his empire,

This sixteenth-century bronze plaque from Benin illustrates the regal qualities of West African kingdoms. The figures standing on either side of the king are not children but the king's attendants. Because they are less important personages, they are represented as smaller than the king. (Courtesy of the Museum of Primitive Art)

the Askia appointed Islamic judges to every large district to administer Moslem justice in place of traditional laws. His own court became the highest court and it heard appeals from the lower courts.

By this time Songhay had become a huge empire characterized by order and prosperity. The vigor of commercial and scholarly activities in the empire served as a tribute to the skill and wisdom of Askia the Great.

SONGHAY'S SOCIAL SYSTEM

The social system in Songhay had many aspects of a caste system; that is, a person's social and economic standing depended largely on what group or tribe he belonged to. If he belonged to a particular group, it often determined what sort of work he did and with whom he associated.

There were special castes whose members specialized in caring for horses. Another caste did most of the smithing, particularly the job of making spears and arrows for the Songhay army. In the lake districts west of Timbuktu, there was a caste of fishermen who transported people and goods at the command of the ruler. Members of other castes and tribes attended to the personal needs of the king, his family and his court.

At the top of the social and political ladder were the descendants of the original Songhay people of Kukya. They enjoyed special privileges and were kept apart from the general population. They were not allowed to marry outside of their own caste.

Next in line were the freemen and traders of the cities and town, and the members of the army, composed of noble cavalrymen, and foot soldiers. A large portion of the infantry was made up of war prisoners.

The Songhay army represented something of an innovation for the western Sudan. Up to this time Sudanese armies had been raised by giving each province a quota for providing a certain number of soldiers. Any male citizen of the empire who was healthy could be drafted into military service. If this citizen happened to be a farmer, his fields would be left to the weeds while he was away.

The Songhay empire eliminated the waste caused by drafting people with civilian occupations. They organized a completely professional army. Members of the Songhay army were expected to fight the wars of the empire, and that was all. In Sunni Ali's time, that was enough to keep them busy all the time.

The Songhay army lived in barracks and camps separated from the civilian population. The mounted soldiers (those who rode horses or camels) were armed with sabres and lances and wore breastplates padded with cotton, for protection. The foot soldiers fought with long, pointed staves and with bow and poison-tipped arrows.

At the bottom of the social scale in Songhay were the war captives and slaves who were not placed in the army but put to work on the farms. Some of the "farms" were rather like labor camps.

Ethiopia and East Africa

❧ INTRODUCTION: Early development in Africa was not limited to the Western Sudan. East Africa also produced great kingdoms, and it maintained a thriving trade with areas as far away as China.

Perhaps the oldest African kingdom—and certainly the most enduring Christian empire the world has seen—is Ethiopia, which traces its orgins to the ancient city of Aksum, founded around 1,000 B.C. Until its recent demise, the Ethiopian kingdom maintained a continuity of almost 3,000 years.

The kingdom came to an end on September 12, 1974, when the last emperor, Haile Selassie, was overthrown by a military coup. The emperor, who traced his lineage back to biblical times, was put under house arrest and died almost a year later at the age of 84.

Other areas of East Africa also developed early. South of Ethiopia, along the coast of present-day Kenya and Tanzania, trading centers flourished more than 2,000 years ago. As early as 800 A.D., the East Coast had contact with India, China, and the countries of the Persian Gulf. One of the most famous cities of that time was Kilwa, which still can be found on the map of Tanzania. Traveling through East Africa in 1331, Ibn Battuta describes Kilwa as "one of the most beautiful and well-constructed towns in the world."

The first selection that follows deals with the history of ancient Ethiopia; the second describes the early development of the East African coast.[8] ❧

ETHIOPIA: AN ANCIENT KINGDOM SURVIVES

Long before the coming of Christ, when Europeans were still fighting petty tribal wars and had not even thought of building cities, Ethiopia was one of the great powers of the world. The ancient Ethiopian kingdom, called Aksum, was an African rival to the famous classical states of the Mediterranean: Athens, Sparta, and Rome.

Haile Selassie, in military dress, was the last Emperor of Ethiopia. He ruled for more than 40 years, carrying on a tradition reaching back 30 centuries. Here, at the Addis Ababa airport in 1971, he bids farewell to Ali Bhutto, the Prime Minister of Pakistan at the time. (Leon E. Clark)

Even before the founding of Aksum, as early as 2500 B.C., Ethiopia was a thriving trading center. The ancient Egyptians referred to it as the land of Punt, or God's land. From this "paradise on earth" came the treasures of the ancient world: ivory, ebony, gold, panther skins, cosmetics, cinnamon, frankincense, and myrrh. Since cinnamon originally came from India, it is clear that the Land of Punt had already established commercial ties with the East.

The origins of Askum—like the traditional histories of all ancient kingdoms—are embedded in a mythical story. According to the *The Glory of Kings*, an official history of Ethiopia, the emperors of Ethiopia were descended from the biblical Queen of Sheba. This famous queen is held to have been the ruler of Ethiopia during the reign of King Solomon of Israel and Judah (974-932 B.C.). The Queen of Sheba is said to have visited Solomon "with a very great train, with camels that bear

spices, and very much gold and precious stones." She bore
Solomon a son, Menilik I, who, according to legend, ruled
Ethiopia and founded the line of the "Lion of Judah." Haile
Selassie, the last Emperor of Ethiopia, claimed the title "King
of Kings, Conquering Lion of Judah, Elect of God."

Traditionally Ethiopia was divided into a number of
semi-independent kingdoms, each with its own ruler. At the
head of these separate kingdoms reigned the "strong man" or
"King of Kings," who represented the most powerful region at
the time.

The story of Solomon and Sheba shows that Ethiopian
kings long considered themselves, and consequently were
considered by others, to be an essential part of ancient history.
They believed themselves to be descendants of the "chosen
people," a term referring to the tribe of Israelites, who
considered their people the "Elect of God."

Because of its central location, the Land of Punt was able
to establish itself as a commercial center very early in the
history of the world. Ethiopia, therefore, had contacts with
Egypt, Greece, Rome, India, and the Middle East. It has been
the center of the development of the world's great religions and
has been influenced by them all. Around 1000 B.C. the Sabeans
of South Arabia invaded the land of Punt in the hope of
profiting from the thriving trade. They settled along the coast
and in the highlands of what is today northern Ethiopia.

Because the Sabeans were Semites, Europeans often claim
that Ethiopians are not Africans but Semites, related to the
ancient Israelites. They cite as evidence the fact that a sizable
Jewish community existed in Ethiopia until recently, and that
the Emperor called himself Lion of Judah, Elect of God.

But the truth is that Ethiopians—even the Falashas, or
black Jews—are very much Africans. The glorious empire of
Aksum developed a very distinctive civilization, with its own
language, script, and remarkable architecture. Aksum's court
structure, its terrace farming, and its monuments were similar
to features found throughout East African ruins. The Ethiopian kingship was also typical of African sacred kingships,

This obelisk from ancient Aksum, called a steale, *stands more than 60 feet high and is carved out of one piece of stone. (Leon E. Clark)*

and the lion is a common African royal insignia. Thus Aksum was a uniquely African empire that incorporated much from the outside and yet developed a distinctive culture of its own.

Aksum is especially significant in the study of African history because it is one of the few African states that developed its own written language. Because of this, historians have been provided with documents that date back at least two thousand years. From these documents we have learned of the advanced form of agriculture practiced by the early Ethiopians; of the flourishing trade with Egypt, the Middle East, India, China, and Rome; and of the great accomplishments and riches of the Ethiopian emperors.

There are also archaeological evidences of Aksum's greatness. The Aksumites constructed numerous towns and trading stations connected by a paved highway from the coast. The towns and cities of Aksum had paved streets for the horses and chariots of the rich. The palaces of the nobility were impressive constructions of stone. Archaeologists have found the ruins of

The monolithic stone church of Lalibela, above, is carved out of the surrounding hill. Notice the size of the man standing below. (Leon E. Clark)

these buildings, as well as the stone relics of mighty temples erected to the gods' honor. The monuments, called *stelae*, or obelisks, are pillars, beautifully carved from one solid piece of stone. One of these still standing at Gondar, is over 70 feet tall, intricately carved and engraved in both Geez (the ancient Ethiopian language) and Greek.

Archaeologists digging in the vicinity of ancient Aksum have also uncovered numerous coins obviously minted by Aksumites over a period of seven hundred years before the birth of Christ. Many of these coins are inscribed in both Geez and Greek, giving evidence of the historic links between these two cultures and of the familiarity that Askum emperors had with Greek literature.

In approximately 330 A.D. Aksum became one of the first ancient kingdoms to accept Christianity as its national religion. And Ethiopia remains Christian today, making it the longest enduring Christian empire. This new religion gave added strength and unity to the empire. It provided a common philosophy that brought the people from the separate Ethiopian kingdoms together, making it possible for the empire to defend itself against outside invasions.

However, during the eighth century, the Muslims invaded Aksum, spurred on by a quest for converts to Islam, their new religion, and also seeking to expand their commercial trade. The Muslims conquered Egypt and thereby isolated Ethiopia from the rest of the Christian world for more than eight hundred years. Although Aksum put up strong resistance, the Muslims were able to capture Ethiopia's coastline and cut off Aksum's access to the Red Sea. Thus, although Aksum was famous throughout the world for its flourishing trade as late as 700 A.D., it lost its old trading ports.

Ethiopian civilization, however, continued to develop. Since it was virtually cut off from trade, the mountainous kingdom turned to agriculture as a source of wealth. Like Europe at the time, Ethiopia lost its long-standing ties with the East and became a feudal kingdom.

This feudal empire developed in isolation from the rest of the world until the fifteenth century. During the years of isolation, the impressive rock-hewn churches, which are now among the wonders of the world, were built. The most famous of these is named after King Lalibela because it was constructed during his reign, in the thirteenth century. It is carved from one huge stone block, hollowed out with perfectly square corners and intricate designs. Lalibela still serves as a church today, and its site has become known as the Jerusalem of Ethiopia. It still attracts pilgrims, some of whom travel hundreds of miles to worship there.

During its isolation, Ethiopia became a land of wealthy nobility, intricate religious ceremonies, and elaborate court rituals. When the Portuguese rediscovered Ethiopia in the fifteenth century, they found it to be a rich and impressive feudal kingdom much like their own. They had been searching for Ethiopia for three hundred years in their quest for the legendary Prester John, who supposedly ruled over a Christian kingdom in the heart of Africa. When they found Christian Ethiopia, they believed it to be this legendary land, and its splendor matched their expectations.

In 1896, when the rest of Africa was conquered by European colonialists, Ethiopia, because of its strong and well-established army, was able to defeat the Italians in the famous battle of Adowa.

Until the overthrow of the Emperor in 1974, Ethiopia maintained feudal traditions that had not changed for hundreds of years. Like Europe in the Middle Ages, Ethiopia had its equivalent of knights and lords, princes, serfs, and royal courts, and a church structure similar to the traditional Roman Catholic Church. As we have seen, Haile Selassie, the last emperor, still claimed the impressive archaic title "King of Kings" and all the ceremonies of the ancient Aksum court remained intact under his rule. Until the revolution of 1974, Ethiopia's people lived as peasants tied to the land as they had for centuries, while the aristocracy and the Church owned the land. Much of this has changed under the new government, but the greatness of Ethiopia's past still lives as a cultural and national legacy.

EAST AFRICAN GLORY

In the year 1331 an educated man from the city of Fez in Morocco traveled down the long east coast of Africa. His name was Ibn Battuta. Along the coast of East Africa he found peace and wellbeing. He passed through many important trading cities and some smaller towns. He was made welcome by rulers and businessmen and teachers. But the famous city of Kilwa pleased him more than any other. "Kilwa," he wrote, "is one of the most beautiful and well-constructed towns in the world."

Today only a shabby village stands there. Yet beyond the village can still be found the walls and towers of ruined palaces and large houses and mosques, which is what Moslems call their churches. A great palace has been dug out of the bushes that covered it for hundreds of years. It is a strange and beautiful ruin on a cliff over the Indian Ocean. Many other ruins stand nearby. But the strangest thing about Kilwa and the towns nearby is that there is little to be found about them in the new history books. Even when the cities are described, they are said to be not African, but the work of people from Arabia or Persia.

History books that say this are out of date, and they are wrong. People who have studied these cities on the east coast say that the cities were an important part of Africa's life between the years 1000 and 1700. And these cities were African, or, to be more exact, Swahili. This is the name of the people of the coast of Kenya and Tanganyika and the island of Zanzibar. [In 1964 Tanganyika and Zanzibar joined to form the Republic of Tanzania.]

The story of these great cities goes far, far back in time. More than 2,000 years ago, at the beginning of the Iron Age in central-southern Africa, small trading villages grew up along this coast. They were marketplaces for the goods traded between East Africa and other countries along the Indian Ocean, especially Arabia. In these trading villages the sailors and traders did business and visited with African friends and families, stayed and lived with them, married and made their own homes. These facts are found in an Egyptian–Greek guidebook on trading and sailing in the east coast waters. The guide was probably written in the first century A.D., which is the time right after the birth of Christ.

About 1,200 years ago, many people from southern Arabia moved to the islands along the east coast of Africa. They brought their Moslem religion with them. Soon they married and made homes among the people of the coast.

At the same time, trade increased all around the Indian Ocean. There were busy seaports all the way from southern China to Kilwa and the nearby cities. Things made in China began to reach Kilwa. East African ivory began to reach China. Trading also went on with India and the countries of the Persian Gulf and Arabia.

Then African people far inland from the Indian Ocean began to offer gold for the things they needed from other countries, the most important of which was cotton for clothing. The cities of the coast took the gold and sold it to other countries. Gold became more important than ivory for trading, though ivory was still in demand. Southeast Africa became as famous for its gold, among the countries of the East, as Ghana was among the countries of the West.

Gold from Mozambique and Zimbabwe, as we now call those countries, began to leave the seaports of East Africa in the tenth century. A few hundred years later the traders of Kilwa had charge of this gold trade. They became very rich. They made all traders from other countries pay heavy taxes on what was sold and bought. Kilwa grew and became a clean and comfortable city.

There were many other big trading cities—big enough to be called city-states or even city-empires because they controlled large areas. There were also many smaller ones. Their rulers were in touch with many large countries of the Far East. Around the year 1400, for example, one African city sent a giraffe to the emperor of China. We know this happened

The broken vaults shown at left are part of the Great Mosque of Kilwa, built in the twelfth and fifteenth centuries by the sultans who controlled this ancient East African trading center, whose location is shown in the map above. (Marc and Evelyne Bernheim from Rapho Guillumette)

because there is a Chinese painting of this giraffe, and the painting has words on it which tell the story of the gift. A few years later the Chinese emperor sent back gifts with a friendly fleet of many ships and thousands of sailors.

The trading that went on across the Indian Ocean was the work of many different peoples. The Swahili were the people on the African side. They were very important in Africa's history. There were Swahili poets who wrote in the Arabic language and in their native language. Storytellers sang of the adventures of famous men. Traders brought fine pots and jars from China and India and Persia and displayed them so that their friends and customers could enjoy seeing them.

Then trouble came to these trading cities. In 1497, Vasco da Gama, a famous sailor from Portugal, sailed around the Cape of Good Hope, which is at the southern end of Africa. Other Portuguese captains who followed Vasco da Gama attacked and robbed city after city. They destroyed the Indian Ocean trade.

The cities on the southeastern coast, especially Kilwa, never really got over this time of pirate raids. The cities of the northern coast came through better. The pirates did not attack them as violently, and in time they were able to grow again.

Later—in the 1700's—the language of the Swahili began to be widely written. Men wrote about the events of their own day. They also wrote about the glories of the past. They were not, we may remember, the only people in Africa writing in their own language. Far across on the other side of Africa, the educated people of the western Sudan were doing the same. If most African people did not know how to write—and, living in close tribal groups, they had no need for writing—it is still important to remember those people who did know how to write and who, like the Swahili people, used this knowledge well.

Part II: The Coming of the European

Introduction

When the Portuguese explorer Vasco da Gama rounded the Cape of Good Hope in 1497, he opened the east coast of Africa to European pillage and exploration. But more than 50 years earlier, Portuguese explorers had sailed down the west coast in search of trade, adventure, and Christian converts.

The Portuguese were the first Europeans to explore Africa. As early as 1440, they had traveled as far south as Cape Blanco (on the northern tip of the coast of Mauritania) only a few days' sail from Portugal. They were primarily interested in the adventure of pushing farther and farther south and in the riches they hoped to amass from African gold and ivory and Asian spices. These same motivations drove most of the European explorers during the Age of Exploration, including the Italian Christopher Columbus whose search for the spices of India landed him in the West Indies in 1492.

By 1485 the Portuguese had sailed as far south as the Congo River, on the West African coast. They had also set up trading forts along the way, the first one as early as 1448. Permanent settlement, as well as exploration, was very much a part of the Portuguese plan.

Besides their commercial interests, however, the Portuguese had another important mission: saving souls. Prince Henry of Portugal, the man behind these explorations, was a devout Catholic, and he pictured his sailors and missionaries as Christian crusaders bringing the word of God to African heathens. He even sought and received the support of the Pope in these activities.

Another dimension to this Christian quest was the search for the land of Prester John. Late in the 12th century, a legend grew in Europe about the existence of a vast, rich empire ruled by a priest named Prester John. Letters about and supposedly by Prester John circulated in Europe. At first Europeans placed this Christian utopia in Asia, but later decided it was in Africa, thus increasing the motivation of Europeans to explore the African coast.

For more than 100 years—from about 1440 to 1550—the Portuguese monopolized trade along the West African coast, dealing mostly in gold, ivory, and pepper. (Notice the location of contemporary Ivory Coast and Ghana, formerly the Gold Coast). But another commodity—slaves—gradually came to rival other goods as the number one export item from Africa.

The Portuguese carried their first slaves aboard ships for sale in European markets in 1441. By the middle of the 16th century, according to one writer, "a vast majority of the inhabitants of the southernmost province [of Portugal] were Negroids, and even up as far as Lisbon, negroes outnumbered the whites. The two races intermingled, resulting in the Negroid characteristics of the Portuguese nation even today."

As significant as the early slave trade was, there was a limit to the number of African laborers Europe could absorb. By the 17th century, however, the situation had changed dramatically. The new colonies in North and South America and the Caribbean had large plantations that required workers, and they looked to Africa to meet their needs.

Responding to the increased demand for African labor, the British, French, and Dutch entered the West African slave trade and began to compete with the Portuguese for a share of the "black gold." From 1440 to 1870, it is estimated that somewhere between 15 to 20 million Africans were lost to the slave trade, many of whom died en route to the African coast or on board ship.

The following selections, almost all first-hand accounts, describe the personal horrors produced by the slave trade as well as the social and economic effects the trade had on Africa.

Slaves, Guns, More Slaves

🎜 INTRODUCTION: One question that always arises when discussing the slave trade is this: how could Africans sell their own people?

To begin with, a form of slavery had existed in Africa for 500 years before the coming of the Europeans, but African slavery was far more humane than what developed under the trans-Atlantic system. Traditional African slaves were usually prisoners of war who were often returned to their own people for a price, but were sometimes sold as slaves to work for others. More often than not, however, such slaves were allowed to earn money, own land, and intermarry with the local population. They also developed skills like boat-building that made them important and therefore accepted members of society. This type of integration never took place under European and American slavery.

Nevertheless, the fact that slavery already existed in Africa made it possible for Europeans to offer merchandise and expect to receive people in return. Some African chiefs and kings sold their prisoners of war to the Europeans; in exchange they often received guns, which greatly added to their power. The chiefs without guns were then put at a distinct disadvantage.

Almost overnight, it became necessary for a chief to possess guns in order to maintain his power. Otherwise his people would be taken by opposing chiefs. And since the guns came from the Europeans, and the Europeans demanded slaves in exchange, more and more African chiefs began to engage in the selling of prisoners. Guns, and therefore slavery, became a necessary part of survival.

In a very real sense, then, Africans were forced by this vicious cycle to sell other Africans.

Moreover, the Europeans competed among themselves for slaves, which escalated the entire enterprise even further. If the English, for example, gave guns to a cooperative chief, then the

80

Dutch, the French, or the Portuguese felt that they had to give guns to their "friends," for otherwise the English would get all the slaves. The net result of this arms race was a great increase in hostilities among Africans. The Europeans, then *increased* warfare; they did not decrease it, as is sometimes thought. More warfare, after all, resulted in more prisoners and therefore more slaves—exactly what the Europeans wanted.

The selection that follows shows the escalation trap that many African traders fell into. The first two parts, "Slaves" and "Guns," are adapted from the writings of William Bosman, a Dutch slave trader who worked in West Africa at the end of the seventeenth century. The last part of the selection, "More Slaves," is adapted from a first-hand account written by a Swedish traveler, C.B. Wadstrom, in the late eighteenth century.[9] ⅍

SLAVES

The first business of one of our traders when he comes to Fida [later called Whydah, the most important slave port of the African west coast] is to satisfy the customs of the African king and leaders. This usually means paying about 100 pounds in Guinea value, after which we have free license to trade, which is announced throughout the whole land by the crier.

But first, before we can deal with any person, we are obliged to buy all of the king's personal stock of slaves at a set price; this is commonly one third or one fourth higher than ordinary. Having done this, we are free to deal with all the king's subjects. But if there happens to be no stock of slaves, the trader must then run the risk of trusting the inhabitants with goods to the value of one or two hundred slaves. The inhabitants then send the goods to the country, sometimes 200 miles inland, to buy slaves at the markets. You should be informed that markets of men here are kept in the same manner as those of beasts with us.

Many of our countrymen [in Holland] fondly imagine that parents here sell their children, men their wives, and one brother the other. But those who think so deceive themselves; for this never happens on any account except necessity or some great crime. Most of the slaves that are offered to us are prisoners of war, which are sold by the victors as their booty.

Elmina castle, located on the coast of Ghana, was built by the Portuguese in 1481 and played a major role in the slave trade. (Leon E. Clark)

When these slaves come to Fida, they are put in prison all together. When we are ready to buy them, they are all brought out together in a large plain where our surgeons examine them thoroughly, even to the smallest detail. All the slaves are forced to stand naked for the examination, both men and women; no distinction is made for the sake of modesty. Those which are approved as good are set on one side; and the lame and faulty are set on the other as *invalides*. The *invalides* are those over 35 years, or those who are maimed in the arms, legs, hands, or feet, or who have lost a tooth, are gray-haired, have films over their eyes, or are afflicted with several other diseases.

The *invalides* and the maimed being thrown out, as I have

told you, the remainder are numbered, and it is recorded who delivered them. In the meantime, a burning iron, with the maker or name of the companies, lies in the fire, ready to put our mark on the slave's breast.

This is done so we may distinguish our slaves from the slaves belonging to the English, French, or others [who also mark their slaves]. This also prevents the Negroes from exchanging bad slaves for good ones, which they are very good at.

I doubt not but this trade seems very barbarous to you, but since it is followed by mere necessity it must go on. But we still take all possible care not to burn them too hard, especially the women, who are more tender than the men.

We are seldom detained in the buying of these slaves, because their price is established, the women being one fourth or fifth cheaper than the men. When we are agreed with the owners of the slaves, they are returned to their prison. From that time on, they are kept at our cost, which is two pence a day a slave. This serves to keep them alive, like our criminals, on bread and water.

To save costs, we send them on board our ships at the very first opportunity. The masters of the ships first strip them of all they have on their backs, so they come aboard stark naked, women as well as men. They are forced to stay in this condition unless the master of the ship is willing (as he often is) to give them something to cover their nakedness.

GUNS

The African military leaders along the coast are highly skilled. 'Tis not unpleasant to see them exercise their army. They lead their men so cleverly, sending them several ways at the same time—sitting, creeping, lying, and so forth. It is really to be admired that they never hurt one another.

Perhaps you wonder how the Negroes come to be furnished with firearms. But you will be astonished when you learn that we sell them incredible quantities. We are giving them the knife to cut our own throats. But we are forced to it, for if we did not, they might be supplied by the English, Danes, or Brandenburghers [Germans]. And if we all agreed not to sell them any arms, the private traders [considered illegal by the trading companies] would furnish them.

Firearms and gunpowder have been the most popular merchandise here for a long time. If we did not supply them, we would not get our share of the trade.

Slave traders are shown here bartering for slaves along the West African coast. Close examination of the slaves as well as branding was part of the process. (Peabody Museum of Salem, MA)

MORE SLAVES

The Moors, who inhabit the countries north of the Senegal River, have a most horrible reputation for their wars of robbery. They cross the river and, attacking the Negroes, carry many of them off. There are many who make a living from such attacks.

The French, to encourage them in this, make annual presents to the Moorish kings. The presents are given under certain conditions: first, that their subjects shall not carry any of their gum to the English, and second, that they shall be ready on all occasions to furnish slaves. To help them fulfill this second condition, the French never fail to supply them with ammunition, guns, and other instruments of war.

To confirm what I have now said, I shall put down the following example:

The King of Almammy had, in the year 1787, very much to his honor, enacted a law forbidding any slave whatever to be marched through his territories. At this time several French vessels lay at anchor in the Senegal, waiting for slaves. The route of the black traders, because of the King's law, was blocked, and the slaves had to be carried to other parts. The French, unable therefore to fill their ships, protested to the King. But the King was not willing to listen, and he returned the presents which had been sent him by the Senegal Company, of which I myself was a witness. At the same time, the King declared that all the riches of that company would not make him change his mind.

In this situation, the French were obliged to turn to their old friends, the Moors. As on previous occasions, the Moors were ready and active. They set off in raiding to surprise the innocent Negroes and to bring them the horrors of war. Many unfortunate prisoners were sent, and for some time continued to be sent in. I was once curious enough to wish to see some of those that had just arrived. I applied to the director of the company, who conducted me to the slave prisons. I there saw the unfortunate captives, chained two and two together by the foot.

A second source of slaves for the Europeans is pillage, which is of two kinds: public and private. It is public when practiced by the direction of the king, private when practiced by individuals. It is practiced by both blacks and whites. This last I call robbery.

The public pillage is, of all others, the most plentiful source, and it maintains and furthers the slave trade. The kings of Africa [whom I have visited] become excited by the merchandise shown them, which consists primarily of strong liquors. Hence they give orders to their military to attack their own villages in the night.

The Story of a Slave

❧ INTRODUCTION: Almost all the accounts we have of the slave trade come from Europeans. As a result, we know more about the business of buying slaves than about the experience of being a slave.

Fortunately, however, a few documents do exist that give an inside view from an African perspective. One of the most famous is *The Early Travels of Olaudah Equiano*, the autobiography of a liberated Ibo slave, written in 1789. The next two readings are taken from this book.

Equiano was kidnapped from his home when he was only 11 years old. The year was 1756; the place was eastern Nigeria. For several months Equiano was passed from African owner to African owner, until finally he was brought to the coast and sold to British slave merchants for the sum of 172 cowries [shells used for money]. He was first shipped to Barbados, in the West Indies, then to Virginia, and eventually to England, where he fought with his master in the Seven Years' War. Because of his service, Equiano thought he would be freed, but when the war ended in 1763, he was sent back to the West Indies. He was then 17 years old.

Fortunately, an American Quaker bought Equiano and made him assistant to a ship's captain. With the captain's help, Equiano was able to develop his own small trading business, and within three years he earned enough money to buy his freedom. The price was 40 pounds. A year later, in 1767, he returned to England, where he became a citizen and a leader in the antislavery movement.[10] ❧

One day, when all our people were gone out to their work [in the fields] as usual, and only I and my dear sister were left to mind the house, two men and a woman got over our walls, and in a moment seized us both; and, without giving us time to cry

87

out or make resistance, they stopped our mouths and ran off with us into the nearest wood. Here they tied our hands and continued to carry us as far as they could, till night came on, when we reached a small house where the robbers halted for refreshment and spent the night.

We were then unbound, but were unable to take any food; and, being quite overpowered by fatigue and grief, our only relief was some sleep, which [eased] our misfortune for a short time. The next morning we left the house and continued traveling all the day. For a long time we had kept to the woods, but at last we came into a road which I believed I knew. I had now some hopes of being [saved]; for we had advanced but a little way before I discovered some people at a distance, on which I began to cry out for their assistance; but my cries had no other effect than to make them tie me faster and stop my mouth, and then they put into a large sack. They also stopped my sister's mouth and tied her hands; and in this manner we proceeded till we were out of the sight of these people. . . .

My sister and I were then separated. . . . At length, after many days' traveling, I got into the hands of a chieftain in a very pleasant country. This man had two wives and some children, and they all [treated] me extremely well and did all they could to comfort me, particularly the first wife, who was something like my mother. Although I was a great many days journey from my father's house, yet these people spoke exactly the same language with us. This first master of mine, as I may call him, was a smith; and my principal employment was working his bellows, which were the same kind as I had seen in my vicinity.

. . . My master's only daughter and child by his first wife sickened and died, which affected him so much that for some time he was almost frantic and really would have killed himself, had he not been watched and prevented. However, in a small time afterward he recovered, and I was again sold. I was now carried to the left of the sun's rising, through many dreary wastes and dismal woods, amidst the hideous roaring of wild beasts. The people I was sold to used to carry me very often

Olaudah Equiano. (New York Public Library, Schomberg Collection)

when I was tired, either on their shoulders or on their backs.

From the time I left my own nation I always found somebody that understood me till I came to the seacoast. The languages of different nations did not totally differ, nor were they so [complicated] as those of the Europeans, particularly the English. They were therefore easily learned; and, while I was journeying thus through Africa, I acquired two or three different tongues. In this manner I had been traveling for a considerable time, when one evening, to my great surprise, whom should I see brought to the house where I was but my dear sister.

As soon as she saw me she gave a loud shriek and ran into my arms—I was quite overpowered; neither of us could speak, but, for a considerable time, clung to each other in mutual embraces, unable to do anything but weep. Our meeting affected all who saw us; and indeed, I must acknowledge, in honor of those [black] destroyers of human rights, that I never met with any ill treatment or saw any offered to their slaves, except tieing them, when necessary, to keep them from running away.

When these people knew we were brother and sister, they [allowed] us to be together; and the man to whom I supposed we belonged lay with us, he in the middle, while she and I held one another by the hands across his breast all night; and thus for a while we forgot our misfortunes in the joy of being together; but even this small comfort was soon to have an end, for scarcely had the fatal morning appeared when she was again torn from me forever! I was now more miserable, if possible, than before. . . .

I did not long remain after my sister, I was again sold, and carried through a number of places, till, after traveling a considerable time, I came to a town called Timnah, in the most beautiful country I had yet seen in Africa. It was extremely rich, and there were many rivulets which flowed through it, and supplied a large pond in the center of the town, where the people washed. . . . I had been about two or three days at [the house of my new master] when a wealthy widow, a neighbor of his, came there one evening and brought her an only son, a young gentlemen about my own age and size. Here they saw me; and, having taken a fancy to me, I was bought from the merchant, and went home with them. Her house and premises were situated close to one of those rivulets I have mentioned, and were the finest I ever saw in Africa: they were very extensive, and she had a number of slaves to attend her. The next day I was washed and perfumed, and when mealtime came, I was led into the presence of my mistress and ate and drank before her with her son. This filled me with astonishment, and I could scarce help expressing my surprise that the young gentleman should suffer me, who was bound, to eat with him who was free; and not only so, but that he would not at any time either eat or drink till I had taken first, because I was the eldest, which was agreeable to our custom. Indeed, everything here, and all their treatment of me, made me forget that I was a slave.

The intricate carving of this sixth-century clay pouring vessel from the Congo indicates the sophistication of the civilization that greeted early European explorer- sin Africa. (Courtesy of the Museum of Primitive Art)

The language of these people resembled ours so nearly that we understood each other perfectly. They had also the very same customs as we. There were likewise slaves daily to attend us, while my young master and I, with other boys, sported with our darts and bows and arrows, as I had been used to do at home. In this resemblance to my former happy state, I passed about two months, and I now began to think I was to be adopted into the family, and was beginning to [become accustomed] to my situation, and to forget by degrees my misfortunes, when all at once the delusion vanished; for, without the least previous knowledge, one morning early, while my dear master and companion was still asleep, I was awakened out of my [dreams] to fresh sorrow, and hurried away. . . .

Thus I continued to travel, sometimes by land, sometimes by water, through different countries and various nations, till, at the end of six or seven months after I had been kidnapped, I arrived at the seacoast. . . .

The first object which saluted my eyes when I arrived on the coast was the sea, and a slaveship, which was then riding at anchor and waiting for its cargo. These filled me with astonishment, which was soon converted into terror, which I am yet at a loss to describe. . . .

When I was carried on board I was immediately handled and tossed up, to see if I were sound, by some of the crew; and I was now persuaded that I had got into a world of bad spirits, and that they were going to kill me. Their complexions, too, differing so much from ours, their long hair, and the language they spoke, which was very different from any I had ever heard, united to confirm me to this belief. Indeed, such were the horrors of my views and fears at the moment that if ten thousand worlds had been my own, I would have freely parted with them all to have exchanged my condition with that of the meanest slave in my own country.

When I looked round the ship too, and saw a large furnace or copper boiling, and multitude of black people of every description chained together, every one of their [faces] expressing dejection and sorrow, I no longer doubted of my fate; and quite overpowered with horror and anguish, I fell motionless on the deck and fainted. When I recovered a little, I found some black people about me who I believed were some of those who brought me on board and had been receiving their pay; they talked to me in order to cheer me, but all in vain. I asked them if we were not to be eaten by those white men with horrible looks, red faces, and long hair. They soon told me I was not. . . .

Soon after this, the blacks who brought me on board went off and left me abandoned to despair. I now saw myself deprived of all chance of returning to my native country or even the least glimpse of hope of gaining the shore, which I now considered as friendly; and I even wished for my former slavery, in preference to my present situation, which was filled with horrors of every kind, still heightened by my ignorance of what I was to undergo. I was not long [allowed] to indulge my grief; I was soon put down under the decks, and there I received such a [smell] in my nostrils as I had never experienced in my life; so that, with the [horrible] stench and crying together, I became so sick and low that I was not able to eat, nor had the least desire to taste anything.

I now wished for the last friend, death, to relieve me; but soon, to my grief, two of the white men offered me eatables; and, on my refusing to eat, one of them held me fast by the hands and laid me across [a large bar] and tied my feet while the other flogged me severely. I had never experienced anything of this kind before; and, although not being used to the water, I naturally feared that element the first time I saw it; yet nevertheless, could I have got over the nettings, I would have jumped over the side; but I could not; and, besides, the crew used to watch us very closely who were not chained down to the decks, lest we should leap into the water: and I have seen some of these poor African prisoners most severely cut for attempting to do so, and hourly whipped for not eating. This, indeed, was often the case with myself.

The Story of a Slave

PART II

ℐ INTRODUCTION: In the first part of "The Story of a Slave," we saw how Equiano was kidnapped, carried overland by a series of African owners, and finally sold to the British on the coast. His treatment under his African masters was quite humane. "Indeed," he says, "everything here, and all their treatment of me, made me forget that I was a slave."

Under the British, however, his condition changed drastically. He was put in the hold of a ship, where the stench and the crying of his fellow captives made him sick; he was flogged for not eating; and, finally, he was driven to the point where he "wished for the last friend, death."

At the same time, Equiano looked back somewhat fondly on his former slave state, and with good reason. Commenting on the condition of slaves in Africa, he says: "How different was their condition from that of slaves in the West Indies! With us they do no more work than other members of the community, even their master. Their food, clothing, and lodging were nearly the same as theirs [the masters'], except that they were not permitted to eat with those who were free-born; and there was hardly more difference between them and freemen than between members of a family and the head of the family. Some of these slaves even have slaves under them as their own property, and for their own use."

Treatment of this sort was never provided by the Europeans or Americans. In part II of "The Story of a Slave," Equiano shows dramatically how the two systems differed. He relates his experience on board ship and his contact with the slave market in Barbados. ᕽ

In a little time after, amongst the poor chained men, I found some of my own nation, which in a small degree gave

94

ease to my mind. I inquired of them what was to be done with us. They told me we were to be carried to these white people's country to work for them. I then was a little revived and thought, if it were no worse than working, my situation was not so desperate: but still I feared I should be put to death, the white people looked and acted, as I thought, [so savagely]; for I had never seen among any people such instances of brutal cruelty; and this not only shown toward us blacks but also to some of the whites themselves. One white man in particular I saw, when we were permitted to be on deck, flogged so unmercifully with a large rope near the foremast that he died in consequence of it; and they tossed him over the side as they would have done [an empty keg].

This made me fear these people all the more; and I expected nothing less than to be treated in the same manner. I could not help expressing my fears to some of my countrymen: I asked them if these people had no country, but lived in the hollow [of] the ship. They told me they did not, but came from a distant [state]. "Then," said I, "how comes it in all our country we never heard of them?" They told me, because they lived so very far off.

I then asked, where were their women? Had they any like themselves? I was told they had. "And why," said I, "do we not see them?" They answered, because they were left behind. I asked how the vessel could go. They told me they could not tell, but that there were cloths put upon the masts by the help of the ropes I saw, and then the vessel went on, and the white men had some spell or magic they put in the water when they like in order to stop the vessel. I was exceedingly amazed at this account and really thought they were spirits. I therefore wished much to be [away from] them, for I expected they would sacrifice me: but my wishes were in vain, for we were so quartered that it was impossible for any of us to make our escape. . . .

At last, when the ship we were in had got in all her cargo, they made ready with many fearful noises, and we were all put under deck, so that we could not see how they managed the vessel. But this disappointment was the least of my sorrow. The stench of the hold while we were on the coast was so terrible that it was dangerous to remain there for any time, and some of us had been permitted to stay on the deck for the fresh air; but now that the whole ship's cargo were confined together, it became absolutely [sickening]. The closeness of the place and the heat of the climate, added to the number in the ship, which was so crowded that each had scarcely room to turn himself, almost suffocated us. This produced [uncontrolled perspiring], so that the air soon became unfit for [breathing] from a variety of [unbearable] smells, and brought on a sickness amongst the slaves, of which many died, thus falling victims to the [inhuman greed] of their purchasers.

This wretched situation was again aggravated by the [chafing] of the chains, now become [intolerable], and the filth of the [toilet] tubs, into which children often fell and were almost suffocated. The shrieks of the women and the groans of the dying rendered the whole a scene of horror almost inconceivable. Happily perhaps for myself I was soon reduced so low here that it was thought necessary to keep me almost always on deck; and [because of] my extreme youth I was not put in [chains].

In this situation I expected every hour to share the fate of my companions, some of whom were almost daily brought upon deck at the point of death, which I began to hope would soon put an end to my miseries. Often did I think many of the inhabitants of the deep much more happy than myself; I envied them the freedom they enjoyed, and as often wished I could change my condition for theirs. Every circumstance I met with served only to render my state more painful and heighten my fears and my opinion of the cruelty of the whites.

One day they had taken a number of fishes; and when they had killed and satisfied themselves with as many as they thought fit, to our astonishment who were on the deck, rather than give any of them to us to eat, as we expected, they tossed the remaining fish into the sea again, although we begged and

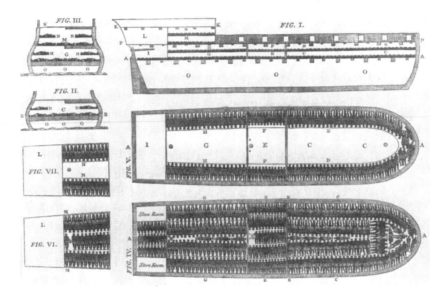

These diagrams of slave ships illustrate the inhuman conditions under which slaves had to exist during the "Middle Passage." The need to use all available space, a purely economic consideration, took precedence over all humane factors. (Peabody Museum of Salem, MA)

prayed for some as well as we could, but in vain; and some of the countrymen, being pressed by hunger, took an opportunity, when they thought no one saw them, of trying to get a little privately; but they were discovered and given some very severe floggings.

One day, when we had a smooth sea and moderate wind, two of my wearied countrymen, who were chained together (I was near them at the time), preferring death to such a life of misery, somehow made through the nettings and jumped into the sea; immediately another quite dejected fellow, who, on account of his illness was allowed to be out of irons, also followed their example; and I believe many more would very soon have done the same if they had not been prevented by the ship's crew, who were instantly alarmed. Those of us that were the most active were in a moment put down under the deck; and there was such a noise and confusion amongst the people of the ship as I never heard before, to stop her and get the boat

out to go after the slaves. . . . Two of the wretches were
drowned, but they got the other, and afterwards flogged him
unmercifully for thus attempting to prefer death to slavery.

In this manner we continued to undergo more hardships
than I can now relate, hardships which are inseparable from
this accursed trade. Many a time we were near suffocation from
the want of fresh air, which we were often without for whole
days together. This, and the stench of the [toilet] tubs, carried
off many. . . .

At last we came in sight of the island of Barbados, at which
the whites on board gave a great shout and made many signs of
joy to us. We did not know what to think of this; but, as the
vessel drew nearer, we plainly saw the harbor, and other ships
of different kinds and sizes: and we soon anchored amongst
them off Bridge Town. Many merchants and planters now
came on board, though it was in the evening. They put us in
separate parcels and examined us attentively. They also made
us jump, and pointed to the land, signifying we were to go
there. We thought by this we should be eaten by this ugly men,
as they appeared to us; and when, soon after, we were all put
down under the deck again, there was much dread and
trembling among us, and nothing but bitter cries to be heard
all the night [because of these fears, so much so] that at last the
white people got some old slaves from the land to pacify us.
They told us we were not to be eaten but to work, and were soon
to go on land where we should see many of our country people.
This report eased us much; and sure enough, soon after we
landed; there came to us Africans of all languages. We were
[led] immediately to the merchant's yard, where we were all
penned up together like so many sheep in a fold, without
regard to sex or age. As every object was new to me, everything I
saw filled me with surprise. . . .

We were not many days in the merchant's custody before
we were sold after their usual manner, which is this: on a signal
given (as the beat of a drum), the buyers rush at once into the
yard where the slaves are confined and make choice of that
parcel they like best. The great noise and clamor, and the

eagerness visible in the faces of the buyers serve . . . to increase the [fear] of the terrified Africans. . . . In this manner, without scruple, relations and friends are separated, most of them never to see each other again.

I remember in the vessel in which I was brought over, in the men's apartment, there were several brothers who, in the sale, were sold in different lots; and it was very moving on this occasion to see and hear their cries at parting. O, you Christians [in name only]! Might not an African ask you: learned you this from your God, who says unto you, Do unto all men as you would men should do unto you?

Is it not enough that we are torn from our country and friends to toil for your luxury and lust of gain? Must every tender feeling be likewise sacrificed to your [greed]? Are the dearest friends and relations, now [made even] more dear by their separation. . . , still to be parted from each other, and thus prevented from cheering the gloom of slavery with the small comfort of being together, and mingling their sufferings and sorrow? Why are parents to lose their children, brothers their sisters, or husbands their wives?

Surely this [separation from relatives] is a new refinement in cruelty. [It gives no advantages to the owner but simply] aggravates distress and adds fresh horrors even to the wretchedness of slavery.

"Ivory First, Child Afterwards"

✏ INTRODUCTION: The slave trade had a profound and devastating effect on Africa, which can be seen even today.

First, it robbed the continent of more than 15 million of its strongest and healthiest men and women. The enormous wealth of this labor was literally stolen from Africa and "deposited" in the "banks" of Europe and America.

Second, it turned African against African. It produced a vicious competition for human life, and it brought guns to make this competition especially violent. The result was an explosion in the size and number of wars in Africa.

Third, it prepared the way for the European takeover during the colonial period. When slaves became the major product of Africa, other products and local crafts suffered. Not only were skilled workers lost to the slave trade itself, but the trade destroyed the incentive to develop cash crops and other sources of wealth, with the result that Africa was left behind other continents in economic development. At the same time, slave wars weakened the various political units of Africa, making them vulnerable to outside control. With a weak economy and weakened armies, Africa was in no position to defend itself against the Europeans.

Finally, and perhaps most important, the slave trade had a brutalizing effect on the African populace as well as on the slaves themselves. The Africans at home saw their countrymen chained, branded, and sold, their villages burned, their cultures disrupted.

The following selection describes the horrors of a caravan carrying slaves from the interior to the coast, in this case the East Coast. The head of the caravan, Tip-pu-Tib, was a powerful and greatly feared Afro-Arab leader who controlled a large kingdom in what is now the eastern Congo.

This selection was written by Albert J. Swann, an Englishman who went to Africa in 1882 as an agent for the London Missionary

Africans captured in the interior were chained or yoked with a forked branch and then marched to the trading stations on the coast. (Jackdaw, London)

Society. By this time the slave trade had been abolished on the West Coast, but it still flourished in the East. Swann's mission, as he explains, was to "cooperate with men and women of various nationalities to undermine and finally destroy the Slave Trade that flourished around the great lakes."

The selection relates to the waning days of the slave trade, but the forced-march technique of transporting slaves that it describes was used throughout Africa for over two hundred years. Sometimes more slaves died than reached the Coast.[11] ❧

. . . We met the notorious Tip-pu-Tib's annual caravan, which had been resting after the long march through Ugogo and the hot passes of Chunyo. As they filed past we noticed many [slaves] chained together by the neck. Others had their necks fastened into the forks of poles six feet long, the ends of which were supported by the men who preceded them. The women, who were as numerous as the men, carried babies on their backs in addition to a tusk of ivory or other burden on their heads. They looked at us with suspicion and fear, having been told that white men always desired to release slaves in order to eat their flesh, like the Upper Congo cannibals.

It is difficult to describe the filthy state of their bodies; in many instances, not only scarred by the cut of the "chicote" [a piece of hide used to enforce obedience], but feet and shoulders were a mass of open sores, made more painful by the swarms of flies which followed the march and lived on the flowing blood. One could not help wondering how many of them have survived the long tramp from the Upper Congo, at least 1,000 miles distant.

The headmen in charge were most polite to us as they passed our camp. Each was armed with a rifle, knife, and spear, and, although decently clothed in cotton garments, they presented a thoroughly villainous appearance.

Addressing one, I pointed out that many of the slaves were unfit to carry loads. To this he smilingly replied:

"They have no choice! *They must go, or die!*"

Then ensued the following conversation:

"Are all these slaves destined for Zanzibar?"

"Most of them, the remainder will stay at the coast."

"Have you lost many of them on the road?"

"Yes! Numbers have died of hunger!"

"Any run away?"

"No, they are too well guarded. Only those who become possessed with the devil try to escape; there is nowhere they could run to if they should go."

"What do you do when they become too ill to travel?"

"Spear them at once!" was the fiendish reply. "For if we did not, others would pretend they were ill in order to avoid carrying their loads. No! We never leave them alive on the road: they all know our custom."

"I see women carrying not only a child on their backs, but, in addition, a tusk of ivory or other burden on their heads. What do you do in their case when they become too weak to carry both child and ivory? Who carries the ivory?"

"She does! We cannot leave valuable ivory on the road. *We spear the child and make her burden lighter.* Ivory first, child afterwards!"

For downright savagery this beat anything I had met with. "Ivory first, child afterwards!" I repeated over and over again. Alas! I was destined many times to witness the truth of that cruel statement.

Thus early in my life I understood what Livingston meant and felt when he wrote the following:

> Besides those actually captured, thousands are killed, or die of their wounds and famine, driven from their homes by the slave-raider. Thousands perish in internecine wars, waged for slaves with their own clansmen or neighbors; slain by the lust for gain which is stimulated by the slave-purchasers. The many skeletons we have seen amongst the rocks and woods, by the pools, and along the paths of the wilderness, all testify to the awful sacrifice of human life which must be attributed directly or indirectly to this trade of hell.

The Triangular Tempest

🖙 INTRODUCTION: The African slave trade was created by forces outside Africa.

The major force was the need for cheap labor on the plantations of North and South America. Acting as a huge economic magnet, this force enslaved millions of men and women, pulled them from the West Coast of Africa, deposited them in the Western Hemisphere, and thereby laid the foundation for the economic development of the Americas. It seems safe to say that American prosperity was partially built on the backs of African workers, who provided much of the needed labor.

The following selection explains the conditions in the Americas that led to the demand for African "help." It then explains the system of trade that supported slavery, providing a good overview of the entire slave-trade issue.[12] 🐦

The slave trade grew big because of European activities in the distant lands beyond the Atlantic.

In 1492, having sailed westward across the Atlantic, Christopher Columbus and his men arrived at some islands of the Caribbean Sea, which lies between North and South America. Knowing nothing of the existence of the American continent (although northern Europeans had in fact reached it many centuries earlier), Columbus believed that he had come near to India. So he called these Caribbean islands the West Indies, a name they still bear. Others followed Columbus. They entered the vast land masses of North, Central and South America.

These others, who were Spanish soldiers and adventurers, ruined the American peoples whom they found. Their intention was not trade, but loot; not peace, but war; not partnership, but enslavement. They fell upon these lands with greed and the fury of destruction. And the American peoples, unlike the Africans, were unable to defend themselves. Being at an earlier stage of social and technical development than the Africans, they fell easy victims to Spanish violence. Along the coast of Guinea, the Portuguese and other Europeans had begun by trying their hands at violence. But they had given that up. The Africans they met were too strong for them. In the Americas it was different.

There was terrible destruction of the "Indians," the name that was mistakenly given by these raiders to the native-born American peoples. A Spanish report of 1518, only twenty-six years after the first voyage of Columbus across the Atlantic, says that when the island of Cuba was discovered it was reckoned to contain more than a million "Indians," but "today their number does not exceed 11,000. And judging from what has happened, there will be none of them left in three or four years' time, unless some remedy is applied."

No remedy was applied, in Cuba or anywhere else; or none that made much difference. Whole populations of enslaved "Indians," forced to work for Spanish masters in mines and on plantations, withered and died, or rebelled and were killed.

Trying desperately to find new sources of free labor, the Spanish began sending out their own people under conditions that were no different from slavery. But they could not find enough of them. Where else to look for slaves? The answer was West Africa. Already the Portuguese and Spanish had imported a few West African captives into their own countries. Now they began to export West Africans to the West Indies and the mainland of the Americas.

In this they faced enormous difficulties. They had first to seize or buy their African captives and bring them back to Spain and Portugal. They had then to get these men across the Atlantic without entirely ruining their health, no small problem in the foul old sailing ships of those days. Lastly, they had to turn these captives, or those who were still alive after the

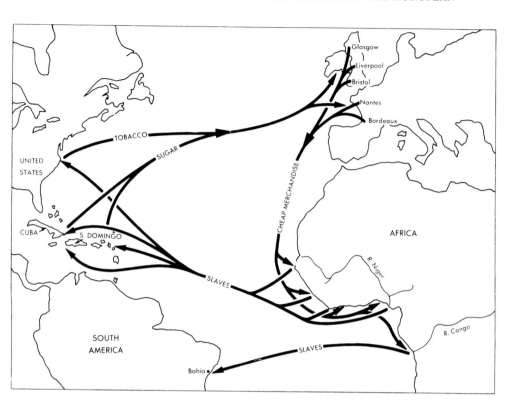

crossing of the seas, into slaves. But this, too, proved very difficult. For the Africans resisted enslavement by every means they could. They broke out in revolt after revolt, led by heroes whose names we shall never know. They fought to the death. They spread fear and panic among the Spanish settlers. They went up into the mountains or deep into the forests and founded free republics of their own. They made history in their fight for freedom.

But Spanish arms and organization, together with the golden profits of the slave trade, proved too strong. In 1515 the Spanish shipped back to Europe their first cargo of West Indian sugar, then a luxury of great price. And in 1518, a grim date in the history of the Atlantic slave trade, the Spanish carried their first cargo of captives directly from West Africa to the West Indies. After that, throughout the sixteenth century, the slave trade grew by leaps and bounds.

It continued to grow in later years. As the wealth and size of the American plantation-colonies became ever larger, so also did the demand for slave labor. There developed what was to become known as the *triangular trade*, a commercial system which greatly helped to build the continued industrial and technical progress of western Europe in the eighteenth and nineteenth centuries.

This new and potent trading system, starting in the late sixteenth century, was called triangular because it had three distinct stages or "sides." Each of these "sides" brought a profit to the merchants and manufacturers of western Europe.

In the first stage or "side" of this trade, merchants in the big ports of western Europe bought and shipped to West Africa goods such as cottons, alcoholic spirits, metalware, and firearms, for sale to African chiefs and kings in exchange for slaves. These slaves were prisoners of war or condemned criminals. If they had stayed in West Africa, they would have been domestic or household slaves . . . [as Equiano was before he was shipped to the West Indies]. African chiefs and kings often exchanged such "slaves" among themselves. They saw no reason for not selling them to Europeans. So it was fairly easy for the Europeans to buy captives.

The second "side" of the triangular trade lay in taking these captives across the Atlantic, usually in chains, and selling them in exchange for sugar, tobacco, rum, and other products to plantation-owners, who turned them into real slaves.

The third "side" consisted in taking the American products back to Europe and selling them at very high prices.

On the Guinea coast the Europeans went on buying gold and other goods. Increasingly, though, they concentrated on buying captives, for the profits of the "triangular trade" became ever greater. The profits became so great that in the eighteenth century the Europeans even brought gold from Brazil to the *Gold Coast* (modern Ghana) in order to buy captives they could not otherwise obtain.

This slave trade enormously enriched the nations of

western Europe. But it made those of West Africa much poorer. Most of this still lay in the future; yet the beginnings of the evil trade were also part of the sixteenth-century scene. The cloud then was no bigger than a man's hand; but soon it grew into a tempest, and the tempest blew and raged for years, even for centuries.

Ending the Slave Trade

❧ INTRODUCTION: The slave trade came to an end for two main reasons: morality and money.

The morality was expressed by Europeans—mostly the English —who recognized the evil of putting other human beings in chains. Beginning around 1750, churchmen in England delivered fiery speeches against the trade, arguing that all people were created equal in the eyes of God. An abolition movement developed in England, antislavery organizations were formed, and in 1807 the British Parliament passed a law making it illegal for British ships to take part in the slave trade. In 1833 parliament abolished slavery entirely in British territories.

Other countries, however, were not quick to follow Britain's lead. In fact, they fought the abolitionist movement. Ships from Spain, Portugal, and the United States continued to transport slaves until the latter half of the nineteenth century. For years English ships patrolled the coast of Africa, trying to prevent what England, much to her credit, regarded as illegal trade. The United States did not abolish slavery until 1863, and Brazil, not until 1888.

The antislavery movement probably could not have succeeded on humanitarian grounds alone, as important as these were. It needed the help of economics. In fact, it can be argued that money was just as important as morality in ending the slave trade. The Europeans at this time were going through the Industrial Revolution. Machines were replacing people, making slave labor less important. Moreover, the machines needed raw materials, much of which came from Africa. Thus it became more profitable to keep the Africans in Africa producing minerals and other raw materials than to send them to American plantations.

Also, Europeans were beginning to think that slave labor did not pay. They accepted the economic theories of Adam Smith, a famous English economist, who argued that free labor was more profitable in the long run because free people work harder and, of course, spend more money, which helps the economy. Furthermore, free workers support themselves, rather than depend on their masters.

All of these reasons, humanitarian and economic, combined to suggest that the slave trade should end. But stopping the trade was not easy. After all, it had become part of the African economic system.

The next selection is taken from a report by an English captain, trying to persuade an African chief from eastern Nigeria to stop trading in slaves. The report was printed in 1848.[13] ❧

King Pepple of Bonny, accompanied by Anna Pepple, his *juju* man [high priest], and Hee Chee, Anna Pepple's secretary, for the first time went on board a man-of-war, for the purpose of paying a visit to Captain Craigie, where he was received with the usual salutes. When the King and his party had finished breakfast, Captain Craigie presented to His Majesty a box containing presents from the English government, which the King desired might be opened.

Captain Craigie then proceeded to read to King Pepple and his party the dispatch of Lord Palmerston dated 14th April, 1838, relative to slave abolition, and strongly impressed upon His Majesty that part which states that treaties had already been made between England and other African princes for the purpose of putting an end to the slave trade, and that in those cases the Articles of Treaty had been faithfully maintained.

Captain Craigie assured the King that England ever dispensed justice and would encourage the lawful commerce of the Bonny in every way; that she would send out ships in abundance for their palm-oil and other products; and if the Bonny men directed their attention properly to these, he was certain they could easily get rich without exporting slaves.
. . .

The King, Anna Pepple, and the *juju* man for some time remained silent; the idea of making such a proposal seemed to them to be incomprehensible. At length Anna Pepple said, "If we cease to sell slaves to foreign ships, our principal source of wealth will be gone; the English were our first customers, and the trade has since been our chief means of support."

Captain Craigie: "How much would you lose if you gave up selling slaves for exportation?"

Anna Pepple: "Too much—very much—we gain more by one slaveship than by five palm-oil ships."

Hee Chee, Anna Pepple's secretary: "We depend entirely on selling slaves and palm-oil for our subsistence; suppose, then, the slave trade done away with, the consumption of palm-oil in England to stop, the crop to fail, or that the English ships did not come to Bonny, what are we to do? We

This painting shows the surrender of a Spanish slave brig to a British ship in 1834. The English tried to enforce their ban on slave trading by patrolling the West African coast. (Peabody Museum of Salem, MA)

must starve, as it is contrary to our religion to cultivate the ground."

Captain Craigie: "There need be no fear of the demand for palm-oil in England ceasing, or of English ships not coming out to the Bonny to take from you your products in exchange for British merchandise; but if you can show clearly that your losses will be so great by giving up slave exportation, I think it possible that the Queen of England may in some measure repay you for your loss."

Juju man: "Suppose a Spanish ship comes to Bonny with goods to exchange for slaves; are we to send her away? This morning you made a breakfast for me, and as I was hungry it would have been foolish not to have eaten; in like manner, if the Spanish ship had things which we stood in need of, it would be equally foolish not to take them."

Captain Craigie: "How would the abolition of slave importation so materially affect you?"

King Pepple: "It would affect myself and chiefs thus— first, by stopping the revenues arising from slaves being exported; second, our own profit on slaves, and that arising from piloting slave ships up to and out of Bonny, would be lost."

Captain Craigie: "I again assure you that the slave trade must be stopped. Not one vessel can escape from the Bonny, as you will know from the *Scout's* blockade of the river in 1836 and 1839. If it becomes necessary, I shall anchor a vessel off Juju Point, and to pass her you are aware will be impossible; but as the English government always adopts the principle of putting an end to evils by friendly agreement rather than by compulsion, and as it is possible that they may be disposed, if your requests are within reasonable limits, to make you an annual repayment for a term of years (perhaps five years), how much would you consider to be sufficient?"

After some consultation among themselves, Hee Chee, Anna Pepple's secretary, said, "The King will take $4,000 yearly."

Captain Craigie: "As I said before, I am not authorized to treat for any sum, but I am certain that $4,000 would be considered too much; indeed, I would not venture to propose more than $2,000. If you say that this sum (for the time above specified) will be sufficient, I shall lay the matter before the English government."

The King, Anna Pepple, the *juju* man, and Hee Chee had a discussion for some time. They for a long while insisted on not naming less than $3,000, till they at last came down to $2,000.

Treaties for Trade

⚜ INTRODUCTION: When European merchants shifted their emphasis from slaves to other goods, they opened up a new era in their relations with Africa: the era of the treaty.

The purpose of the treaty was to make sure that merchants had stable markets. A European nation would sign an agreement with an African chief, who promised to trade only with that country. Quite often the treaty would go beyond purely business matters, calling for the establishment of Christian missions or allowing the European country to send soldiers to the area. In many cases the Africans did not realize what they were agreeing to.

The treaty that follows was signed on March 19, 1877, concluding an agreement between England and the King of Mellella, River Congo.[14] ⚜

Leicester Chantrey Keppel, Esquire, Commander of her Britannic Majesty's ship *Avon,* and Senior Officer of the River Congo, on the part of Her Majesty the Queen of Great Britain and Ireland, Empress of India, &c., and the King of Melella, whose name is hereunto subscribed on the part of himself, his heirs, and successors, have agreed upon the following Articles:

1. The export of slaves to foreign countries is forever abolished in my territory.

2. No European or other person whatever shall be permitted to reside in my territories or those of my heirs or successors for the purpose of carrying on in any way the traffic in slaves.

3. If at any time it shall appear that the slave trade is being carried on through or from any part of my territories, the slave

114

trade may be put down by force.

4. The subjects of Her Britannic Majesty and all white foreigners may always trade freely with my people.

5. In the event of any British or other foreign vessels running aground in any part of the River Congo near to my territory, I faithfully promise that I will in no way allow them to be interfered with.

6. Should any British or other foreign vessel, being aground in the river, apply to me for assistance, I promise to render her all help in my power, provided I am fairly paid for my trouble.

7. Should the ships be attacked by pirates or plunderers, I promise assistance by sending my people with arms, and doing all in my power to punish the robbers.

8. If at any time a naval officer of Great Britain shall require guides or armed people to accompany the said officer against pirates or other enemies of the Queen of Great Britain, I promise to provide them.

9. I declare that no human being shall be sacrificed on account of religious or other ceremonies, and that I will prevent the barbarous practice of murdering prisoners of war.

10. Missionaries or other ministers of the Gospel are to be allowed to reside in my territory.

11. In consideration of these engagements, all past offenses of King Mellella against the Queen of Great Britain, &c., are hereby forgiven.

Concluded on board Her Majesty's ship *Avon*, at Mellella, this 19th day of March, 1877.

> Leicester C. Keppel, Commander, H.M.S. *Avon*
> Mellella, King of Mellella, River Congo
> (His mark)

Witnesses to signatures of Contracting Parties:
> Andrew W. Rogers, Senior Lieutenant, H.M.S. *Avon*
> Henry J. Ollard, Assistant Paymaster, H.M.S. *Avon*
> Capeta of Mellella
> The Sister of Queen Annazoza   their marks

Part III: The Colonial Experience

Introduction

For approximately 350 years—from 1450 to 1800—European traders in Africa remained on the coast of the continent; as long as goods and slaves were brought to them by African traders, there was no need to penetrate the unknown interior. Even when explorers, who by 1850 had mapped most of Africa, brought back stories of the riches of the interior, Europeans were not enticed into colonial expansion.

However, a series of events within Europe finally led to the "scramble for Africa." First, King Leopold of Belgium, eager to increase his wealth and prestige, sent the American explorer Henry Stanley to the Congo to make treaty arrangements with local chiefs. Stanley was so successful that by 1884 Leopold could claim an area in the center of Africa that equalled the size of all Western Europe.

Second, Otto von Bismarck, Chancellor of the German Empire, made a similar thrust into the continent. His agents, in only 18 months between 1883 and 1885, were able to carve out territories in Tanganyika (now Tanzania), Southwest Africa, Togoland, and the Cameroon. Unlike Leopold, however, Bismarck was not so much interested in wealth as in politics. He hoped that his move would draw other European powers into Africa, create competition between England and France (Germany's enemy), and thus improve Germany's position at home.

1884

The other European powers did become alarmed by the Belgian and German moves; they feared that these nations would use their African territories as pawns in the power struggle in Europe. None of them, of course, wanted to be left out, so the rush for African colonies was on.

A conference was called in Berlin in 1884-1885 to lay down the rules of the game (no slave trading, no interference in the territories of other European powers, etc.), and by 1900 the competition was virtually over; almost all of Africa had been

1900-1910

Legend:
- British (B)
- French (F)
- German (G)
- Italian (I)
- Anglo-Egyptian
- Spanish (S)
- Portuguese (P)
- Belgian
- Turkish Vilayets (T)
- Independent
- • "Footholds" or Trading Stations

sliced up and parcelled out by European powers. Only two states escaped colonization: Ethiopia and Liberia.

The scramble for Africa, then, was mostly the result of internal European politics. But once the colonies were established, other factors, such as economics, became increasingly important. With the development of industry in the nineteenth century, European factories needed more and more raw materials. And with the end of the slave trade, Europe looked more and more to Africa to supply these materials. Africa was rich in palm oil, cotton, cocoa, rubber, diamonds, gold, and other minerals. The surest and cheapest way for Europe to get these materials was to control the land that produced them and the people who worked the land. The result was colonialism.

Another factor in the growth of colonialism had nothing to do with money. It concerned the minds and hearts (and souls) of people. For centuries Christian missionaries had been active in Africa, particularly during the antislavery movement of the early nineteenth century. When the European colonies were established, the missionaries saw an even greater opportunity to spread the word of God. They established churches, schools, and hospitals, and as a result became an important part of the colonial apparatus. From their own point of view, however, the missionaries were bearers of civilization, bringing the light of truth to the "dark continent." Many Europeans shared this view; in fact, they felt it was the "white man's burden" to bring the "benefits" of European culture to the "backward" peoples of the world. As Rudyard Kipling, the English poet, wrote in 1899:

> Take up the White Man's burden—
> Send forth the best ye breed—
> Go bind your sons to exile
> To serve your captives' need;
> To wait in heavy harness,
> On fluttered folk and wild—
> Your new-caught, sullen peoples,
> Half-devil and half-child.

The Africans, of course, had a different view of themselves. But they were confronted with the presence of the Europeans and were subjugated to a new political authority, a new economic system, and a new culture and religion. How did they react? How were they affected? What was it like to be an African living under European control? Part III attempts to answer these questions—and to raise others.

"Too White, Like a Devil"

❧ INTRODUCTION: There were many adjustments that Africans had to make under colonial rule, but the first and most obvious one was to the physical appearance of the colonialists. Although Africa and Europe had had trade relations for more than four centuries, very few Africans had ever seen a white person before the beginning of the colonial era.

This selection tells how one African chief reacted to seeing a white man for the first time. The encounter took place around 1890 in what is now Ghana. Bear in mind that white skin is a sign of illness in Africa, and that evil spirits are often depicted as white.

The author of the work from which this reading is adopted, C.C. Reindorf, was the son of an African mother and a European father. He worked as a Christian minister in Ghana and wrote one of the first accounts of traditional West African history, *History of the Gold Coast and Asante*, published in 1895.[15] ❧

King Firempong had charge of Christiansborg, a Danish trading center. All the trade with the Danish merchants was placed in his hands. But he had never seen a white man. In fact he used to hear from traders that Europeans were a kind of sea-creature.

He therefore expressed his desire to see a European, and Mr. Nicolas Kamp, a bookkeeper, was ordered to go to Da, the capital of the Kotokus, to be seen by King Firempong. A grand meeting was held for his reception. In saluting the assembly, Mr. Kamp approached the king and took off his hat; when Mr. Kamp was bowing to salute him, Firempong thought he was an animal who would jump upon him. The king fell down flat from his stool and cried loudly for his wives to assist him.

The drummer and the government interpreter did their best to convince the poor king that Mr. Kamp was a human being and that his movements were the mode of Europeans in paying their respect to superiors. The king got up from the ground and sat on the stool, and ordered his wives to sit between him and the European. By this he could cool down his fears.

Upon seeing the cue—a tail-like twist of hair—down the back of Mr. Kamp (as people were then in the habit of wearing, as the Chinese do nowadays), he said, "Dear me, all animal have their tails at the extremity of the trunk, but Europeans have theirs at the back of their heads!" The interpreters explained to him that it was no tail but twisted hairs. All this while, the king's wives were watching every movement of Mr. Kamp to know whether he was a man or an animal. Not being satisfied yet with all he had seen, the king requested Mr. Kamp to take off his clothes, which he declined to do, saying he would do that only at home, when no lady was present.

The meeting retired and Mr. Kamp went to his quarters, where a table was prepared for him. During the meal, the king's wives stood by peeping at him. Some said, "He eats like a man, really he is a human being!" Finally, Mr. Kamp took off his clothes before old Firempong, who now could touch him. "Ah, you are really a human being, but only too white, like a devil!"

That Was No Welcome
and
"That Was No Brother"

✻ INTRODUCTION: When different cultures meet for the first time, misunderstandings are bound to develop. What members of one culture see in a particular act members of another culture may not see at all. A friendly gesture in one culture may turn out to be a hostile gesture in another. Such misunderstandings were common in the early contacts between Europeans and Africans and, indeed, persisted throughout the colonial period.

The next two selections illustrate this point by describing the same event from two perspectives. In the first selection, Henry Stanley, the famous American journalist and explorer, explains how he was "welcomed" by Africans while exploring the Congo River in the early 1870's with several canoe loads of African companions. Stanley was the first white explorer to trace the entire course of the Congo.

In the second selection, the African chief Mojimba, who led the welcoming party for Stanley, describes how he perceived the encounter. He told his story some years later to a Catholic missionary, Father Joseph Fraessle, who supports Mojimba's claim that such a welcome was friendly and the usual way of greeting strangers.[16] ✺

THAT WAS NO WELCOME

About 8 A.M. we came in view of a marketplace, near which there were scores of small canoes. The men at once rushed into them and advanced all round us. We refrained a long time, but finally, as they became emboldened by our stillness and began to launch their wooden spears, which they proceeded to do all

125

together as soon as somebody cried out *"Mutti"* (sticks), we were obliged to reply to them with a few shots, which compelled them to scamper away ahead of us. Drums then awakened the whole country, and horns blew deafening blasts. Some canoes boldly followed us.

We came, about 10 A.M., to another market green. Here, too, warriors were ready, and again we had recourse to our weapons. The little canoes with loud threats disappeared quickly down river: the land warriors rushed away into the woods. We did not wish to hurry, because the faster we proceeded the quicker we found we were involved in trouble. We therefore loitered indifferently: rest was so rare that it became precious when we obtained it.

At 2 P.M. we emerged out of the shelter of the deeply wooded banks and came into a vast stream, nearly 2,000 yards across at the mouth. As soon as we entered its waters, we saw a great fleet of canoes hovering about in the middle of the stream. The canoe men, standing up, gave a loud shout when they saw us and blew their horns louder than ever. We pulled briskly on to gain the right bank when, looking upstream, we saw a sight that sent the blood tingling through every nerve and fiber of our bodies: a flotilla of gigantic canoes bearing down upon us, which both in size and numbers greatly exceeded anything we had seen hitherto!

Instead of aiming for the right bank, we formed a line and kept straight downriver, the boat taking position behind. Yet after a moment's reflection, as I noted the numbers of the savages, the daring manner of the pursuit, and the apparent desire of our canoes to abandon the steady compact line, I gave the order to drop anchor. Four of our canoes made believe not to listen, until I chased them to return to the line, which was formed of eleven double canoes, anchored ten yards apart. The boat moved up to the front and took position 50 yards above them. The shields were next lifted by the noncombatants, men, women and children in the bows, and along the outer lines, as well as astern, and from behind these the muskets and rifles were aimed.

This engraving, done in 1878, depicts the battle between Henry Stanley and Chief Mojimba on the Congo River in the early 1870's. (Harper Brothers)

We had sufficient time to take a view of the mighty force bearing down on us and to count the number of the war vessels. There were 54 of them! A monster canoe led the way, with two rows of upstanding paddles, 40 men on a side, their bodies bending and swaying in unison as with a swelling barbarous chorus they drove her down toward us.

In the bow, standing on what appeared to be a platform, were ten prime young warriors, their heads gay with red feathers: at the stern, eight men with long paddles, whose tops were decorated with ivory balls, guided the monster vessel; and dancing up and down from stem to stern were ten men, who appeared to be chiefs.

The crashing sound of large drums, a hundred blasts from ivory horns, and a thrilling chant from 2,000 human throats did not tend to soothe our nerves or to increase our confidence. However, it was "neck or nothing." We had no time to pray or to take sentimental looks at the savage world, or even to breathe a sad farewell to it. So many other things had to be done speedily and well.

As the foremost canoe came rushing down, its consorts on either side beating the water into foam and raising their jets of water with their sharp prows, I turned to take a last look at our people and said to them:

"Boys, be firm as iron; wait until you see the first spear, and then take good aim. Don't fire all at once. Keep aiming until you are sure of your man. Don't think of running away, for only your guns can save you."

The monster canoe aimed straight for my boat, as though it would run us down; but when within fifty yards off, it swerved aside and, when nearly opposite, the warriors above the manned prow let fly their spears and on either side there was a noise of rushing bodies. But every sound was soon lost in the ripping, crackling musketry. For five minutes we were so absorbed in firing that we took no note of anything else; but at the end of that time we were made aware that the enemy was reforming about 200 yards above us.

Our blood was up now. It was a murderous world, and we felt for the first time that we hated the filthy, vulturous ghouls who inhabited it. We therefore lifted our anchors and pursued them upstream along the right bank until, rounding a point, we saw their villages. We made straight for the banks and continued the fight in the village streets with those who had landed, hunting them out into the woods, and there only sounded the retreat, having returned the daring cannibals the compliment of a visit.

"THAT WAS NO BROTHER"

When we heard that the man with the white flesh was journeying down the Lualaba (Lualaba-Congo) we were open-mouthed with astonishment. We stood still. All night long the drums announced the strange news—a man with white flesh! That man, we said to ourselves, has a white skin. He must have got that from the river-kingdom. He will be one of our brothers who were drowned in the river. All life comes

This Yoruba wood carving from Nigeria suggests how Africans see the white colonialist—determined, armed, and big-nosed. (American Museum of Natural History)

from the water, and in the water he has found life. Now he is coming back to us, he is coming home. . . .

We will prepare a feast, I ordered, we will go to meet our brother and escort him into the village with rejoicing! We donned our ceremonial garb. We assembled the great canoes. We listened for the gong which would announce our brother's presence on the Lualaba. Presently the cry was heard: He is approaching the Lohali! Now he enters the river! Halloh! We swept forward, my canoe leading, the others following, with songs of joy and with dancing, to meet the first white man our eyes had beheld, and to do him honor.

But as we drew near his canoes there were loud reports, bang! bang! and fire-staves spat bits of iron at us. We were paralyzed with fright; our mouths hung wide open and we could not shut them. Things such as we had never seen, never heard of, never dreamed of—they were the work of evil spirits! Several of my men plunged into the water. . . . What for? did they fly to safety? No—for others fell down also, in the canoes. Some screamed dreadfully, others were silent—they were dead, and blood flowed from little holes in their bodies. "War! that is war!" I yelled. "Go back!" The canoes sped back to our village with all the strength our spirits could impart to our arms.

That was no brother! That was the worst enemy our country had ever seen.

And still those bangs went on; the long staves spat fire, flying pieces of iron whistled around us, fell into the water with a hissing sound, and our brothers continued to fall. We fled into our village—they came after us. We fled into the forest and flung ourselves on the ground. When we returned that evening our eyes beheld fearful things: our brothers, dead, bleeding, our village plundered and burned, and the water full of dead bodies.

The robbers and murderers had disappeared.

Now tell me: has the white man dealt fairly by us? Oh, do not speak to me of him! You call us wicked men, but you white men are much more wicked! You think because you have guns you can take away our land and our possessions. You have sickness in your heads, for that is not justice.

King Ja Ja, Business Whiz

❧ INTRODUCTION: Colonialism is usually given credit for bringing modern technological culture to Africa. It is true, of course, that the Europeans built modern schools and hospitals, introduced scientific techniques of agriculture and industry, improved communications and transportation, and in general infused modern Western culture into traditional societies. But is it true that Africa needed colonialism in order to get these things?

A number of scholars today would say no. They argue that Africa would have modernized anyway through normal trade contacts with Europe, which had gone on for centuries. In fact, these scholars argue, Africa would have developed faster without colonialism because it would have developed naturally, and with its own interests in mind. As it turned out, under colonialism, Africa modernized according to European plans, which seldom put the interests of Africa first.

For example, all the top decision-making positions in colonial Africa were held by Europeans; hence Africans did not develop administrative skills. The entire colonial educational system was designed to produce a supply of clerks and other low-level helpers, not leaders. At the same time, the economics of African colonies was geared to serve European interests, not to give African states a well-balanced income. If, for example, Ghana could grow cocoa, or Tanzania sisal, then that is what these countries grew, nothing else. They were forced to have one-crop economies that could collapse overnight if other countries began to grow the same crop and the total production was more than the world could buy. At the same time, industry was not developed in Africa because the colonial powers wanted to maintain their monopoly in industry, using Africa simply as a source of raw materials and a market for European manufactured goods. The real profits from the raw materials of Africa, then, went into European pockets. As a result, an African middle class—the

131

businessmen in the economy—never had a chance to emerge.

The selection that follows illustrates this last point. King Ja Ja was an Ibo trader from Bonny, an area of contemporary Nigeria just east of Benin, where trade with Europe had existed since the sixteenth century. For three hundred years before that, slaves had been the major export of the region, but with the abolition of slavery and the development of Western industry in the nineteenth century, palm oil became the most important item of trade. Quite literally, palm oil greased the machines of Europe.

In 1861 the head of the Annie Pepple clan, Elolly Pepple, died, leaving his kin in great debt; he owed the British no less than 1,500 barrels of oil. Consequently, no one wanted to assume the leadership of the clan. Finally Ja Ja was elected, at the age of 42, because he was such an excellent businessman. The Ibos still regard him as one of their heroes.

The following selection is adapted from the writings of C.N. de Cardi, a European trader who knew West Africa well during the latter half of the nineteenth century.[17] ❧

Ja Ja had not been head of the Annie Pepple House for many months before he began to show the old chiefs what kind of metal he was made of. During the first twelve months he had selected from among the late Elolly's slaves no fewer than eighteen or twenty young men who had already accumulated a little wealth and whom he thought capable of being trusted to trade on their own. He therefore bought canoes for them, took them to the European traders, and got the Europeans to loan goods to each of these young men. Ja Ja himself stood as guarantor for them.

This operation had the effect of making Ja Ja popular among all classes of the slaves of the late chief. At the same time, the slaves of the old chief of the House began to see that there was a man at the head of the House who would set a good example to their immediate masters, hoping that perhaps their own masters would also trust them. Some of the young men Ja Ja sponsored are now wealthy chiefs in Opobo.

Two years after Ja Ja was placed at the head of the House, the late Elolly's debts were all paid off. Ja Ja saw to it that all the white traders received their payments by the date he had

An old photograph showing Ja Ja with his four wives and one of his daughters. (Leon E. Clark)

promised. Because of the prompt manner in which Ja Ja had paid up, he received, from each ship which the late chief had dealt with, a present varying from 5 to 10 per cent of the amount paid.

From this date, Ja Ja never looked back. He became the most popular chief in Bonny among the white men and the idol of his own people. However, he was looked upon with jealously by the Manilla Pepple House.[This jealousy finally led to a vicious war between the rival Houses of the Annie Pepple and the Manilla Pepple, made even more brutal by the supply of British arms. Ja Ja quickly realized that his fortunes did not lie in Bonny and in 1870 moved a few miles inland and established his own state, called Opobo.]

Opobo became, under King Ja Ja's firm rule, one of the largest exporting centers of palm oil in the delta. For years, King Ja Ja enjoyed popularity among the white traders who visited his river. But the time came when the price of palm oil fell to such a low figure in England that the European firms in Opobo could not make both ends meet. They therefore told King Ja Ja that they were going to lower the price they paid him for palm oil in the river. He replied by ignoring these traders and shipping large quantities of his oil directly to England, permitting his people to sell only a small portion of their produce to the white men stationed on the river.

Ja Ja found, however, that sending his oil to England was not quite so profitable as he could wish. He found that it took too much time to get his returns back from England (at least three months), whereas when he sold in the river he could get three to four times the returns during the same period.

In the meantime, however, the English on the river joined forces and agreed to divide all the produce coming down the river equally among themselves, thereby eliminating competition among the white men. Ja Ja tried several different schemes in order to break up this new monopoly of the white men. At last he hit upon the bright idea of offering the whole of the river's trade to one English trading house.

He hoped that by making an agreement with one rich English house he would be able to restore competition between the white men and thereby make more profit. His bait took with one of the European traders who could not resist the golden vision of the profitable yellow grease (palm oil); Ja Ja had very cleverly convinced him that all the rewards from the hundreds of canoes filled with oil would be his if he would only agree.

A bargain was struck between Ja Ja and the trader, and so one fine morning all the other white traders woke up to find that their monopoly was at an end. They found out through their usual methods. Palm-oil traders would never be caught without a pair of binoculars and a tripod telescope to closely observe their opponent's doings. And one morning, while they

Ja Ja's grandson, the Paramount Chief of Apobo, presides over the 100th anniversary of the founding of Apobo in 1971. (Leon E. Clark)

were taking their usual "spy" around the river, they saw a fleet of over a hundred canoes around their "friend's" wharf. From that time onward, for nearly two years, this separatist trader scooped all the trade.

The fat was now in the fire, and the other traders boldly sent a notice to Ja Ja that they intended to go to his markets. Ja Ja replied that he held a treaty, signed in 1873 by Mr. Charles Livingstone, Her Britannic Majesty's Consul. This treaty empowered him to stop any white traders from establishing trading posts anywhere above Hippopotamus Creek, and allowed him to stop and hold any vessel for a fine of 100 barrels of oil.

In the meantime, clouds had been gathering around the head of King Ja Ja. His wonderful success had kept him from recognizing that he was, in the eyes of the English government, merely a petty African king. He did not allow himself to see that times were changing in the Oil Rivers and that his rights were limited by the new English order. He did not realize, therefore, that when he signed the new protectorate treaty of December 19, 1884, the sixth clause was crossed out. As a result, the new treaty did not allow him to keep white men from proceeding to his markets as the Treaty of 1873 had.

Unaware of this, Ja Ja got himself into a series of disputes with the white traders. This led to his removal from the Opobo River in September 1887, by her Britannic Majesty's new Consul, Mr. H.H. Johnston. Ja Ja was taken to Accra, where he was tried before Admiral Sir Hunt Grubbe, who condemned him to five years' deportation to the West Indies, making him an allowance of about 800 pounds per year.

Poor Ja Ja did not live to return to his country and his people whom he loved so well and whose conditions he had done so much to improve.

The Coming of the Pink Cheeks

PART I

❧ INTRODUCTION: In the last selection, we saw how the European control of trade prevented Africans from developing their own middle class. Businessmen like Ja Ja never had a chance to express their talents. As a result, Africans became dependent upon Europeans; they were more hindered than helped by the so-called material benefits of colonialism.

Even more serious than the Europeans' control of African trade, however, was their control of the land. Most Africans make their living from the soil. More important, they consider land to be a "sacred" part of nature and a traditional part of their heritage. Land is not a commodity that can be bought and sold; it is a gift from God that belongs to everybody, like the air we breathe.

After many generations—and sometimes after centuries—an ethnic group becomes identified with a particular area. The land is their "property," belonging not only to the living members but also to the ancestors who worked the land in the past and to the unborn children who will work the land in the future. When the Europeans came and "bought" land, many misunderstandings developed, for the Africans never meant to "sell" what in their eyes could not be sold.

In the following selection, Chief Kabongo, a Kikuyu from Kenya, describes what happened to his people when the Europeans took control of Kikuyu land. In his lifetime—from the 1870's to the 1950's—Chief Kabongo saw the sharp changes that took place after the coming of the Europeans.[18] ❧

For some years my eldest son had been going to a school kept by some Pink Cheeks only two hours' journey away. These were not the White Fathers, to whom my brother had gone, but were quite different. They wore clothes like the Pink Cheeks who farmed, and many of them were women. They had a medicine house where there were many ill people; there were good medicine-men and good things were done and sick people were made well. Every day my son would go before the sun was high and would come back before the sun set. Then he would eat and fall asleep, too tired to sit around the fire and be told the stories and history of our people or hear of the work that had been done or learn the customs and ways of our people and their laws and conduct. . . .

It was in these days that a Pink Cheek man came one day to our Council. He came from far, from where many of these people lived in houses made of stone and where they held their own Council.

He sat in our midst and he told us of the king of the Pink Cheeks, who was a great king and lived in a land over the seas.

"This great king is now your king," he said. "And this land is all his land, though he has said you may live on it as you are his people and he is as your father and you are as his sons."

This was strange news. For this land was ours. We had bought our land with cattle in the presence of the Elders and had taken the oath and it was our own. We had no king, we elected our Councils and they made our laws. A strange king could not be our king and our land was our own. We had had no battle, no one had fought us to take away our land as, in the past, had sometimes been. This land we had had from our fathers and our fathers' father, who had bought it. How then could it belong to this king?

With patience, our leading Elder tried to tell this to the Pink Cheek and he listened. But at the end he said, "This we know. But in spite of this, what I have told you is a fact. You have now a king—a good and great king who loves his people, and you are among his people. In the town called Nairobi is a council or government that acts for the king. And his laws are your laws." . . .

Like colonialism itself, this white officer travels on the backs of Africans. (Brown Brothers)

For many moons this thing was much talked of by us. Then, when no more Pink Cheeks came and things went on as they had always been, we spoke no more.

Sometimes we heard of strange happenings, or even saw them ourselves, but for the most part life was still as it had always been. The Iron Snake, which I had never seen, had come and had carried men on it, not of our people; then a big path was made through the country half a day from our land. It was wide enough for three elephants to walk abreast. And stones were laid on it and beaten flat, so that grain could have been threshed there.

As the years passed and more and more strange things happened, it seemed to me that this path or road was a symbol of all changes. It was along this road now that came news from other parts; and along it came the new box-on-wheels that made men travel many days' journey in one day and that brought things for the market that the women wanted to have, clothes or beads to wear and pots for cooking. Along this road the young men went when they left to work with the Pink

Cheeks and along it too they went when that day came that they traveled to fight in the war over the sea that the Pink Cheeks made against each other.

It was along this road that many did not come back and some came with no legs, or who could not see. Two of my sons went and only one came back, and he brought only one hand and many strange new ideas and tales. Along the road, too, went the trees that men cut down when they made more and more farms. Without trees to give shade the ground was hot and dry and food grew not well.

By the time that my father, Kimani, died and his spirit joined those of our ancestors, our own land was poor too. For even though many of our family had gone away to work for the Pink Cheeks, our numbers had increased and there was no room for the land to rest and it was tired. The food it grew was poor and there was not enough grown on it for all to eat. Those of our family who worked for the Pink Cheeks sent us food and coins that we could buy food with, for else we could not live.

Little by little, too, the rains fell less. When I was a boy I remember the rains came in plenty twice every year, the little rains and the big rains, and on the hottest days there would be heavy dews, for the trees kept the land cool.

Now it was different; now the little rains had gone and the big rains had become little rains. The big rivers had become little ones and dried up in the hottest time, and I saw this was not good.

Now that my father, Kimani, was dead, I had been chosen Muramati of our *mbari*. I was also now a Ceremonial Elder, a member of the Sacrificial Council.

It seemed to me that Ngai was tired of us. He sent so little rain. We must ask him to look upon us again and must sacrifice a ewe to please him.

I spoke of this one evening, and the Elders said it was good to make sacrifice, for the time of rain had long passed. So the day was fixed and I was chosen to be the leader.

Little Kabongo, my eldest grandson, who bore my name according to our custom, sat with us; he spoke then as do the

The colonialists took control of local African economies and shaped them to serve their own purposes. (Photoworld, Inc.)

young age group today before their elders, but which when we were young we did not.

"This is good," he said. "For three weeks the Pastor at the Mission School has prayed for rain."

"Which will send rain, do you think, the God of the Pink Cheeks or Ngai?" asked a small boy.

"Neither," announced a young man, son of one of my brothers, who was a schoolteacher. "I have read in books that it is the trees that make the rains come. Now that the trees are cut down there is no rain. In the Sacred Grove on the hills there is rain."

The small boy was listening, full of wonder.

"And who makes the trees grow? Surely that is God," said my grandson. "For the Pastor says that God made everything, that God is greater than Ngai."

Such discussions among the young were frequent, and to hear them made me sad. For this new learning seemed to pull this way and that way so that no one knew what was right.

But all this talk did not make more food nor bring us rain.

As there was now so little land and we were so many, the boys as they became men would go away, some to work on farms for the Pink Cheeks, some to a new kind of school-farm for men, where they learned the new customs and also some curious ways; for these grown men were made to play games like little boys, running after balls which they threw. This they did instead of good work.

Munene, one of my younger brothers, had been one of these. He had been away a long time, and when he came back he wore clothes like a Pink Cheek and he came with one of them, in a box-on-wheels, which is called motor-car, along the new road.

The Pink Cheek called a Council together and when all, both Elders and the young men, were assembled and sat round, he spoke. He spoke of Munene; he told us of his learning and of his knowledge of the customs of the Pink Cheeks and of his cleverness at organizing.

"Because of this," he said, "and because he is a wise man, the Government, the Council of Muthungu that meets in Nairobi, have honored him and, in honoring him, are honoring you all."

He paused and looked around at us. Beside him Munene stood smiling.

"He has been appointed Chief of this district and he will be your mouth and our mouth. He will tell us the things that you want to say and he will tell you the things that we want to say to you. He has learned our language and our laws and he will help you to understand and keep them."

We Elders looked at each other. Was this the end of everything that we had known and worked for? What magic had this son of my father made that he who was not yet an Elder should be made leader over us all who were so much older and wiser in the ways of our people? It was as if a thunderbolt had fallen among us.

The Coming of the Pink Cheeks

PART II

🌿 INTRODUCTION: When the Europeans took control of the land, they struck a blow at the traditional sources of authority and leadership. How could Kabongo, for example, lead his people when he did not control the land that fed them? How could he ask them to follow traditional ways when the Europeans could offer greater rewards for following new ways?

Leadership and authority in any society depend upon the ability to meet the needs of the people. Leaders will maintain their authority only as long as they can reward their followers. Even dictators who rule by force must be able to reward the armies that serve them. 🍂

The Pink Cheeks went on.

"Your new Chief will collect the tax on huts, and choose the places for the new schools that you will build everywhere, so that your children may be taught to read and write. He will raise the money for that from you all. I have spoken." . . .

When the Pink Cheek had gone there was much talk. We asked Munene to tell us how this had come about and why he was set above the Elders in this way.

"It is because they do not understand our laws and Councils," he told us. "Because I speak their language and because when I went away in their wars I had many medals."

The medals we knew about, for we had seen them. Many had them.

We spoke then of the tax on huts. It was heavy, for some men had many huts. Those men who had gone to work on the

farms of the Pink Cheeks sent us money, but this we needed to
buy food. More men, therefore, must go.

Munene gave us some good advice. He told that men were
wanted in Nairobi to build the new houses made of stone, both
for the Pink Cheeks to live in and where they sat to make
business and trading. Our men could go there and earn coins
and then they could come back when they had plenty.

This was good, for in this way we would pay our tax and
no man would be taken by the Pink Cheeks for not paying. So
our young men went away down the new road, we were left to
grow what food we could, and all was as usual . . .

It was while these men were still away to make money for
our hut tax that ten of our people came back from the farms
where they worked. They were not needed, they said, there was
no work for them there. With many others, they had been sent
back without money and without food, because there were bad
people who troubled the land.

This was the beginning. Along the new road had come big
boxes-on-wheels that they called lorries [trucks], in which they
had carted logs from the forest. Now these came filled with
people. Many had no homes, for their land had gone to the
Pink Cheeks. Some had no homes because their land had gone
to be mined for gold. We could not let them starve, so we took
them on our land. . . .

It was the end of the dry season and there was little food
left in the storehouses. Our *mbari* had now grown big, and all
these newcomers on our land must eat too. Altogether there
were 1,200 people on the 200 acres of land my grandfather's
father had bought. There was not enough room to grow all the
food.

In the dry season many goats and cattle had died for want
of water. The harvest had been thin and there was little left, and
there was no money to buy food; the last had gone for our hut
tax. I heard the crying of children and I saw the women weaken
in their work. The old men would sit near their huts, too feeble
to walk.

Wangari, whose once-strong breasts hung like empty bags

Europeans trained Africans to become policemen and soldiers to serve colonial purposes, often requiring them to fight against other Africans. (Photoworld, Inc.)

and whose eyes were deep in her head, came to me where I sat by my hut.

"Kabongo, son of Kimani," she said, sitting close, "we women are tired; there is no food and the children are hungry; the young men have no stomachs and the old men are withering as dry leaves. You yourself are weak or before this you would have taken counsel with the Elders. Speak now, for our people wait to hear your word."

I was roused. What she said was true. This was no time to sit and wait. We must hold Council.

The Council met again under the Mugomo tree. There were few, for the new laws of the Pink Cheeks had forbidden big meetings. I looked round at my friends and was sad. Their faces were anxious and their skin was loose on their bones. Even Muonji, who always used to joke, had no smile. For each one had been hungry for many days, and each one told the same story. Everywhere there was a shortage of food, for there was no land and all the time people were being sent back from distant parts. There was uneasiness and some of our tribesmen were troubling our people too much because they wanted to drive the Pink Cheeks from our country. This the Elders told in Council and were uneasy, for we wanted no war with the Pink Cheeks; we only wanted land to grow food.

"We must ask the Council of the Pink Cheeks to lend us some of the land we had lent to them," said one who came from a place where there was land held by the government for future farms and not yet in use.

All agreed that this would be good and for Munene, who as Chief was our spokesman, we made a message to give to the Governor. What we told to Munene he made marks with and, when we had finished, he spoke it to us again and it was good. . . .

Munene took our message and he took also a gift of honey and eggs and went away down the long road and left us to wait.

We waited many days, with hope. It was a whole moon before Munene came back. He came to us slowly and sadly, and we knew from his way that the news was bad.

"They will not give the land," he said. "They say they have no more land for us."

And he told us many things that were not good; he told us of rebellions of some of our people, bad men who took our laws and ceremonies and degraded them; of the Pink Cheek warriors and of some he called Police who did unjust things to our people, who took good men and loyal to the Queen away from their work, and after much useless talk, sent them to live on this land where there is no food.

So I am sitting before my hut and I wait. For soon the time will come for me to creep away into the forest to die. Day by day my people grow thinner and weaker and the children are hungry; and who am I, an old man, to eat the food that would come to them?

As I sit I ponder often of the ancient prophesy of Mogo wa Kebiro. Has the Pink Cheek brought good to my people? Are the new ways he has shown us better than our own ways?

Something has taken away the meaning of our lives; it has taken the full days, the good work in the sunshine, the dancing and the song; it has taken away laughter and the joy of living; the kinship and the love within a family; above all, it has taken from us the wise way of our living in which our lives from birth to death were dedicated to Ngai, supreme of all, and which, with our system of age groups and our Councils, insured for all our people a life of responsibility and goodness. Something has taken away our belief in our Ngai and in the goodness of men. And there is not enough land on which to feed.

These good things of the days when we were happy and strong have been taken, and now we have many laws and many clothes and men dispute among themselves and have no love. There is discontent and argument and violence and hate, and a vying with each other for power, and men seem to care more for disputes about ideas than for the fullness of life where all work and live for all.

The young men are learning new ways, the children make marks which they call writing, but they forget their own language and customs, they know not the laws of their people, and they do not pray to Ngai. They ride fast in motorcars, they work fire-sticks that kill, they make music from a box. But they have no land and no food and they have lost laughter.

The Hut Tax War

❧ INTRODUCTION: The Europeans ruled by force in Africa. Their most powerful political weapon was the rifle. But, as we saw in the last reading, they also gained and maintained control by undermining the old order. By taking over the land, running the schools, and offering jobs in the new colonial government, the Europeans were able to usurp the political power formerly held by the African chiefs. If the Europeans controlled the means of success, if they had the ability to give or withhold rewards, then they also had the power to exact compliance from the people.

Once the Europeans established a colony, they began to exert their political power by demanding taxes from the people. The most common form of taxation, instituted in almost all of the European colonies in Africa, was the hut tax, the price Africans had to pay for living in their own houses. Besides helping to support the new government, this tax made sure that labor was available for the colony's needs: building railroads, building European homes, working on plantations, and generally serving the needs of the Colonialists. The tax forced Africans to take these jobs because there was no other way to earn money to pay the tax. It also forced the workers to migrate to places where work was available—that is, needed. In short, the hut tax made the Africans the servants of the Europeans.

As can be imagined, the hut tax was not popular, and it often led to conflict. In 1888, in the British colony of Sierra Leone, it led to war. The strong-arm tactics of the tax collectors aroused the people and the "war boys" went on a rampage, killing not only many Europeans but also those of their fellow Africans who paid the tax, particularly the Creoles. Not only were the Creoles mulatto (half-white) and therefore identified with the Europeans, but they were in a better position than other Sierra Leoneans to pay the tax because the Europeans favored them with jobs.

The following selection contains the testimony of two Creole women who survived the war. They gave their report to Sir David Chalmers, a British commissioner sent to investigate the situation.[19] ⛬

EVIDENCE OF MRS. TAYLOR

My name is Nancy Violette Taylor. I am a Sierra Leonean. We lived at Bolian on the Mapelle River, Kassi Lake. The policemen's treatment gave rise to this war. When they were sent to collect the tax, they used to ill-use the natives and took their wives. The policemen went to Kabomp and met a man with his wife and daughter. They beat the man and assaulted the wife and daughter, and threatened his daughter with a knife if she cried out. In the town where we were, Captain Carr spent three days. The police caught all the fowls in town.

Q. *Did nobody complain to Captain Carr?*

All the people ran away while Captain Carr was there, till he had left. Captain Carr asked for the Head Chief. He said he would burn the town if the headman did not come. Mr. Smith brought the man to the town, and he promised to pay the tax in a week's time. The next day a messenger, Williams, came to say he must pay in three days' time. He asked Mr. Schlenker to lend him the money.

We were afterwards caught by the war-boys, and I was with them for six weeks. On 29th April a sudden attack was made on Bolian. We went away in a boat, my husband, myself, a constable, and several others. In less than half an hour we got to a town, and over 200 people came on us with cutlasses, sticks and guns. They rushed on the policeman, W.J. Caulker, and chopped him and killed him and took his gun, and then threw him into the sea. They took the other two men and laid them side by side on the ground and chopped them to pieces. They killed my husband at my feet.

I asked them, "Why do you punish Sierra Leoneans so?" They say, "You pay the hut tax." They say, "The Sierra Leoneans with Bai Bureh had not paid the tax, so we did not kill them." They said we were lucky not to be caught before, as the Head Chief had, just the day before, said that no more women were to be killed. They said to me afterwards, "The government say we must not keep slaves, nor have women palaver [womanizing], nor pledge human beings, We say, 'All right.' They come, last of all, and say we must pay for these dirty huts.

"The Government look on us as a lazy people, but the whole of us will die before we pay this tax. We will kill Captain Carr, and then the Governor will come; we will kill the Governor, and then the Queen will come herself. The policemen catch our big men and flog them. If they have not anyone to fight for them they must fight for themselves."

It was one of the war-boys who told me all this.

EVIDENCE OF MISS HUGHES

My name is Miriam Deborah Hughes, daughter of Joseph Elias Hughes [a Creole minister]. The war fell on Thursday; that night we all got inside the mission-house, and a man came to tell us we must leave or we should all be killed.

We then went to Mokombo, where Farma took care of us. Mr. Hughes was not at the station when the war fell; he had gone to Bonthe to borrow some money. On Friday morning we wanted to return to the mission, but Farma told us to stay. Three of the mission men came and called Farma aside and told him about the war. Mammy asked Farma what they had been telling him about. He said, nothing about the war. The mission boy came up and caught hold of me. I told him to let me go. He said, "We are war-boys." They carried us to Momasa and put us inside a house.

The war people used to call me and hold out their hands and mock and tell me to take the money to my mother to give to Governor Cardew. Most of them used to come every day, mocking about the tax. On Thursday night we heard my father's voice on the wharf, which was only a few yards off, but we could not see him out of the house. He said, "Friends, kill me one time, don't punish me too much." I saw his body after; the people would not allow me to go to it, and the water carried it away.

*Africans were forced by the Europeans to pay taxes for living in their own huts.
(Photoworld, Inc.)*

On Saturday they took three women and killed them at the water side. One man took us off and told us he was going to kill my mother for the tax, and they killed her. Then they took me to Tanninahu. Then after that, people told me every day that it was the hut tax that made them kill Creoles, because they joined the English, who had done away with slavery and woman palaver.

Rhodes Steals "Rhodesia"

✣ INTRODUCTION: In most cases, Europeans gained control of their African colonies by signing treaties with local chiefs. Seldom, however, did the chiefs understand what they were signing. As a result, the Europeans were able to take more than the Africans thought they were giving.

Such tactics were used by Cecil Rhodes, the nineteenth-century British imperialist who made a fortune from African diamonds. (Rhodes scholarships to Oxford University are still financed from his estate.) In 1888, Rhodes sent one of his agents, Charles D. Rudd, to southern Africa to negotiate a treaty with King Lobengula of Matabeleland. Rudd, under Rhodes's instructions, offered to give Lobengula 1,000 rifles, 100,000 rounds of ammunition, and a monthly payment of 100 British pounds, and to sell him a gunboat for 5,000 pounds. In exchange, Rhodes would receive "complete and exclusive charge over all metals and minerals situated and contained in the Kingdom."

Lobengula signed this treaty, thinking that he was simply providing Rhodes with "a piece of ground to dig." Rhodes interpreted the treaty differently and took control of the entire kingdom. He never did give Lobengula the money and merchandise that was promised. The kingdom eventually became the British colony known as Rhodesia. In 1965 Northern Rhodesia became the independent state of Zambia, and in 1980 Southern Rhodesia became the nation of Zimbabwe.

The following selection describes the way in which Rhodes tricked Lobengula. The first section is a mock trial of Rhodes's agent as it might have been conducted by Cecil Rhodes's father, a churchman in England. No such trial ever took place, but the ideas expressed in it are valid. The second section gives Lobengula's side of the story. In a sense, he is on trial too, as *his* father does the interrogating. The entire selection is taken from a novel, *On Trial for*

My Country, by Stanlake Samkange, a contemporary scholar and politician. Although the book is fictional, it is based on historical documents.[20] ⅄

THE RUDD CONCESSION

REV. RHODES: "Do you mean to say, Mr. Rudd, that you gave the impression to Lobengula that by signing your concession he was entering into some kind of a treaty in which he could call on the Queen if he were attacked by Boers [Dutch settlers in South Africa] or Portuguese?"

MR. RUDD: "Yes, sir, we gave just that impression."

"But was that a correct impression?"

"In theory, no. We had no power to commit the Queen like that, but in practice, yes. If, for instance, the Boers had tried to interfere in any way with Lobengula, the British Government would for different reasons not have allowed them. This is the point we made."

"I see! You meant that Britain would, for her own selfish ends, let us say, not allow the Matebele to be molested, because in actual fact she was only waiting for an appropriate opportunity to molest them herself?"

"That is correct."

"You did not, of course, commit Britain to not molesting Lobengula."

"No, we did not."

"And, naturally, you did not make this clear to Lobengula. As a matter of fact, you deliberately created the opposite impression in his mind. You made it appear to him that implicit in this treaty was the fact that the British would not attack him, did you not?"

"Yes, we did. I made him take that for granted."

"And yet, as a matter of fact, with Britain's connivance, only a few years later you attacked Lobengula and took his country. Is that not correct?"

"Yes, that is correct."

"Was that not a dishonest and dirty thing for Christian men to do?"

"I am afraid it was, but then, I never professed to care very much for Christianity, nor indeed do I believe that most Englishmen do, except in such matters as being christened, married and buried."

"I see. Is the Rev. Helm here?"

(Thompson answered, "Yes, he is here.")

"Will he come forward, please?"

(A reverend gentleman in clerical collar stepped forward to the altar rails.)

"Are you the Rev. Charles D. Helm, a minister ordained by the London Missionary Society?"

"Yes, sir, I am."

"Is it true that during the time you served as an interpreter at Lobengula's court, you were secretly in the employ of my son, Cecil Rhodes?

"It is."

"Did you tell Lobengula this?"

"No, I did not."

"Why?"

"I did not see anything to be gained by telling him."

"Is it true that Lobengula took pains to pay particular attention to your advice on the subject of a mineral concession in his country?"

"It is true, he did."

"Is it true that he listened to your advice so attentively because he believed you to be impartial in the matter?"

"I think he did."

"Why, then, did you not, in all honesty, let him know that the impartiality he was ascribing to you was misplaced?"

"Because there was nothing to be gained by doing that, and furthermore, my views were not necessarily colored by the fact that I was employed by your son."

"But you were not free to express any other views but those of your employer."

"That may be so. But it also just happened that my employer's views were also my views. So I honestly expressed them."

"Don't you think, then, that in appearing to be impartial when you were not, you were in fact dishonest?"

"No, I do not. I never told Lobengula that I was impartial. If he ascribed impartiality to me that was his own business."

"But you knew him to be doing this and permitted him to do so."

"Yes, I did, because there was nothing to be gained by telling him otherwise."

"You keep on saying this as if your morality is based on gain."

"No, it is not. It is based on prudence, and that means doing what is right and, if people ascribe to me motives that I do not have (such as, for instance, that I am a minister of the Gospel because I thought it was an easy life), . . . [I ignore] them and continue to do what is right."

"And what was right in this case?"

"What was right in this case was that the Matebele power should be broken completely. I believed this to be the will of God. We labored for more than twelve years before we baptized our first convert to the Christian faith in Matebeleland. This was due to the fear of Mzilikazi and his son Lobengula. Since their regime stood between men and God, it was necessary for the regime to be removed."

"And you did not care how the regime was removed?"

"I cared. I would not have had them murdered, for instance, but I was quite prepared to let them walk into a trap that would eventually remove them for the scene."

"So you explained the concession in a manner that made them walk into the trap."

"I put such an interpretation on the concession as they were capable of understanding. After all, I did not fully understand the document myself."

"And since you wanted Lobengula to sign the concession —your interpretation was a favorable one."

"Yes, it was."

"You did not, for instance, tell them that the document in no way committed Britain to defending them in case of attack by, say, Khama?"

"I did not."

"You did not tell them that Britain herself was left free to attack them whereas they were required to keep the peace?"

"I did not."

"You did not draw their attention to the fact that the phrase 'together with full power to do all things that they may deem necessary to win and procure same' could be construed in a manner disadvantageous to them?"

"I did not."

"So you told them only what you wanted them to know, although they thought you were telling them everything. Since you wanted their power broken, even by being led into a trap, what you in fact told them was such as led them to the signing of the concession, which just happened to coincide with the wishes of those who paid you to do just that."

"Yes."

"A remarkable story. An even more remarkable missionary."

ATTEMPT TO STOP INVADERS WITH WORDS

Lobengula continued . . .

"I told the Queen these words. 'Lodzi [Rhodes] paid me money for which I gave him a piece of ground to dig. If you have heard that I have given my whole country to Lodzi, it is not my word. It is not true. I have not done so. Lodzi wants to take my country by strength.'

"I reminded the Queen that her words to me were that I was to send to her when I was troubled by white men. I told her that I was now in trouble and wanted her to help me control these children of hers.

"I received this reply from the Queen. 'The Queen assures Lobengula that the men assembled by the British South Africa Company are not assembled for the purpose of attacking him, on the contrary, are assembled for a peaceful object, namely searching for gold. They were ordered to travel at a distance from the Matebele *kraals* [villages] and always to recollect that

Lobengula. From an early photograph. (Mansell Collection)

Lobengula is the friend of the Queen and that the Queen wishes to maintain peace and friendship with Lobengula.' This is the reply I received from the Queen. She spoke words of peace and yet her *impi* [army] was waiting at my doors with guns and bullets.

"I also sent a word to the *impi* at Macloutsie. I asked them, 'Has the King killed any white men that an *impi* is collecting on his border? Or have the white men lost anything they are looking for?" The answer I received was that the men were a working party, protected by soldiers who were going to Mashonaland along the road already arranged with me. Since I did not know of any such arrangement, I sent another letter to the *impi* and told them that I had made no agreement with anybody about a road to Mashonaland. I also said that all I knew was that Jameson could dig a hole near Tati and nowhere else. I said that if Jameson had thought that by Tati I meant Mashonaland, he was mistaken.

"The *impi* replied to me with these words. 'The *impi* must march on because of the orders of the Queen!' But is this not the same Queen who had told me that she was my friend and wanted to live in peace with me?

"I called together all my *impis* and told them to get ready for war. I ordered them to wait for my word. My *impis* were very keen to bathe their spears in the blood of the white man, but I decided to wait. I did not want to fight."

* * *

Mzilikazi interrupted, "Wait a minute. When you saw the white men's *impi* gathering at Macloutsie, you protested to the Queen and asked why she was doing this when you were joined together, that is, allied, is that right?"

"Yes, that is so, my father."

"Although the Queen told you that these men were assembled for a peaceful purpose and that she wanted to live in peace with you, it was clear to you that these men were in fact, an *impi* and not just peaceful travellers."

"That is so indeed, my father."

"There was no doubt in your mind what the gathering of an *impi* at Macloutsie meant, because you told the Queen that Rhodes wanted to take your country 'by strength'."

"That is so, my father."

"Why, then, did you not stand up to Rhodes and prevent him from taking your country by strength? Why did you not fight?"

"I thought that if I appealed to the white men's sense of justice and fair play, reminding them how good I had been to them since I had never killed or ill-treated a white man, they might hear my word and return to their homes."

"And when you saw that your words were falling on deaf ears, what did you do?"

"I sent another message and told them that I had not given them the road to Mashonaland."

"Yes, and they replied and told you that they had been given the road by their Queen and would only return on the orders of their Queen. What did you do then?"

"I mobilized the army and told them to wait for my word."

"Did you give that word?"

"No."

"Were the soldiers keen to fight?"

A memorial to Cecil Rhodes in Cape Town, South Africa, symbolizes the dominance Rhodes gained over southern Africa. (Photoworld, Inc.)

"Yes, they were dying to fight."

"Why did you not let them fight?"

"I wanted to avoid bloodshed and war."

"I see. A king of the Amandebele, who was born, bred, and lived only to spill blood of men, now did not want to spill blood. Was it only the white man's blood or all blood that you did not want to spill?"

There was silence.

"You heard my question. Answer me, Lobengula."

"I did not want to spill white men's blood."

"Why?"

"Because I wanted to be friends with them."

"Is that so? What did you do to be friends with them?"

"Nothing. I just did not kill them."

"And you allowed them to flout your word as king of the Amandebele? You let them have their way: march up to Mashonaland after you had told them as king, not to go? Is that right?"

"Yes. Because I knew we could never defeat the white man in battle."

"If that is so, why did you not do something to become their friend? Why did you not, like Khama, seek their protection and declare your country a British Protectorate?"

"I was afraid of the effect such a move would have on my people, particularly the *majaha*. I knew that they would have opposed it and might have taken up arms against me."

"So, fear of the *majaha* or a civil war prevented you from doing what you knew you should have done to save your country."

"Yes, I knew that if I fought the white men I would be beaten. If I sought the white man's friendship and protection, there would be opposition to me or civil war. So I decided to pretend to the white men that if they came into the country I would fight, and hoped that they would be afraid and not come. When they called my bluff and came, I decided first to keep quiet."

"Was there no other way out of your dilemma?"

"I did consider marrying the Queen, but even though I hinted at this several times no one followed it up."

"I see!"

Leopold, the Janitor

✣ INTRODUCTION: What effects did colonialism have on Africans? More specifically, how did taxation, forced labor, and other aspects of colonialism change the lives of the people? The answers to these questions vary from colony to colony. In some colonies, the presence of the Europeans had very little immediate effect; in others, it led to great disruption and even atrocities.

In the Congo (now Zaire), the effects were extreme. King Leopold of Belgium, whose claim to much of central Africa prompted the Berlin Conference of 1884-85, assumed personal control of the Congo Free State and exploited its natural resources for his private gain. In particular, he extracted large amounts of rubber by virtually enslaving the human labor need to do the job.

For his part, Leopold claimed that his intentions in Africa were "humane and benevolent," that his agents in the Congo performed a "noble and elevated" task, that they "had to carry on the work of civilization in Equatorial Africa." Writing to his men in the Congo in 1897, he said, "I am glad to think that our agents . . . always bear in mind the rules of the honorable career in which they are engaged. Animated with a pure sentiment for patriotism, recking [caring] little of their own blood, they will care all the more for the natives who will find in them the powerful protectors of life and property, the kindly guardians they need so much."

But outside observers in the Congo found these "kindly guardians" to be anything but "protectors of life and property." Roger Casement, an Irishman working for the British government, went to the Congo in 1903 to investigate conditions there. What he found was forced labor and oppressive taxation, brutally enforced, that rendered the people little better than slaves.

King Leopold denied Casement's charges, but public opinion in Europe forced Leopold to appoint an impartial commission to investigate the Congo affair. The commission, consisting of a

Belgian, an Italian, and a Swiss, visited the Congo in 1904 and found conditions to be just as bad as Casement had reported. As a result, in 1908 the Belgian government wrested control of the Congo from Leopold.

Two years earlier, in 1906, the American journalist and novelist Richard Harding Davis visited the Congo. The following selection, from Davis' book *The Congo and Coasts of Africa*, expresses the author's opinion of Leopold's rule in Africa.[21] ❧

In trying to sum up what I found in the Congo Free State, I think what one fails to find there is of the greatest significance. To tell what the place is like, you must tell what it lacks. One must write of the Congo always in the negative. It is as though you asked: "What sort of a house is this one Jones has built?" and were answered: "Well, it hasn't any roof, and it hasn't any cellar, and it has no windows, floors, or chimneys. It's that kind of a house."

When first I arrived in the Congo the time I could spend there seemed hopelessly inadequate. After I'd been there a month, it seemed to me that in a very few days anyone could obtain a painfully correct idea of the place and the way it was administered. If an orchestra starts on a piece of music with all the instruments out of tune, it need not play through the entire number for you to know that the instruments are out of tune.

The charges brought against Leopold II, as King of the Congo, are three:

1. That he has made slaves of the twenty million blacks he promised to protect.
2. That, in spite of his promise to keep the Congo open to trade, he has closed it to all nations.
3. That the revenues of the country and all of its trade he has retained for himself.

Anyone who visits the Congo and remains only two weeks will be convinced that of these charges Leopold is guilty. In that time he will not see atrocities, but he will see that the natives are slaves, that no foreigner can trade with them, that in the interest of Leopold alone the country is milked.

He will see that the government of Leopold is not a government. It preserves the prequisites and outward signs of government. It coins money, issues stamps, collects taxes. But it assumes none of the responsibilities of government. The Congo Free State is only a great trading house. And in it Leopold is the only wholesale and retail trader. He gives a bar of soap for rubber and makes a "turnover" of a cup of salt for ivory. He is not a monarch. He is a shopkeeper.

And were the country not so rich in rubber and ivory, were the natives not sweated so severely, he also would be a bankrupt shopkeeper. Were the Congo properly managed, it would be one of the richest territories on the surface of the earth. As it is, through ignorance and cupidity, it is being despoiled and its people are the most wretched human beings. In the White Book containing the reports of British vice-consuls on conditions in the Congo from April of last year to January of this year, Mr. Mitchell tells how the enslavement of the people still continues, how "they" (the conscripts, as they are called) "are hunted in the forest by soldiers, and brought in chained by the neck like criminals." They then, though conscripted to serve in the army, are set to manual labor. They are slaves. The difference between the slavery under Leopold and the slavery under the Arab raiders is that the Arab was the better and kinder master. He took "prisoners" just as Leopold seizes "conscripts," but he had too much foresight to destroy whole villages, to carry off all the black man's livestock, and to uproot his vegetable gardens. He proposed to return. His motive was purely selfish, but his methods, compared with those of Leopold, were almost considerate. The work the State today requires of the blacks is so oppressive that they have no time, no heart to labor for themselves.

How much Leopold cares for the material welfare of the natives is illustrated by the price he paid the "boys" who worked on the government steamer in which I went up the Kasai. They were bound on a three-month voyage, and for each

King Leopold II of Belgium made the Congo his "private domain."
(Belgian Consulate General)

month's work on this trip they were given in payment their rice and 80 cents. That is, at the end of the trip they received what in our money would be equivalent to $2.40. And that they did not receive in money but in "trade goods," which are worth about 10 per cent less than their money value. So that of the $2.80 that is due them, these black boys, who for three months sweated in the dark jungle cutting wood, are robbed by the King of 24 cents. One would dislike to grow rich at that price.

The fact that Leopold has granted to American syndicates control over two great territories in the Congo may bring about a better state of affairs, and, in any event, it may arouse public interest in this country. It certainly should be of interest to Americans that some of the most prominent of their countrymen have gone into close partnership with a speculator as unscrupulous and as notorious as is Leopold, and that they are to exploit a country which as yet has only been developed by the help of slavery, with all its attendant evils of cruelty and torture.

That Leopold has no right to give these concessions is a matter which chiefly concerns the men who are to pay for them, but it is an interesting fact.

The Act of Berlin expressly states: *No Power which exercises, or shall exercise, sovereign rights in the above-mentioned regions shall be allowed to grant therein a monopoly or favor of any kind in matters of trade.*

Leopold is only a steward placed by the Powers over the Congo. He is a janitor. And he has no more authority to give even a foot of territory to Belgians, Americans, or Chinamen than the janitor of an apartment house has authority to fill the rooms with his wife's relations or sell the coal in the basement.

White Man's Cotton

☼ INTRODUCTION: When the Europeans came to Africa, they brought more than a new way of making a living. They also brought a new way of looking at the world. Africans exposed to Western education and Christian beliefs developed attitudes that conflicted sharply with their own traditions. They became men of two worlds, uncomfortable in both. Forced labor, evil as it was, never had the lasting impact of the cultural changes brought by colonialism.

The following selection illustrates some of the psychological conflicts suffered by Africans under European control. It tells of a young man from the Congo, Masoudi, who learned some of the white man's ways by leaving his village to work for the Belgians and attend a mission school. When he returned to his native village six or seven years later, he felt out of place. He considered his own people "backward" and "superstitious;" they considered him a little crazy, a man with the "Evil Eye." When the Belgians decided to force the Africans in the area to grow cotton, Masoudi was the logical choice to lead the project. The story, which is true, opens when the Belgian administrator arrives in Masoudi's village to break the news to the people.[22] ☼

It was not long after Masoudi's marriage that [the village of] Ndola received a visit from the administrator himself. He asked the chief, Matungi, to call the village together. When everyone had assembled, the Bwana Mkubwa [white man] told them that from now onwards they must all plant certain crops in addition to those they normally planted. Cotton was the chief innovation. He explained that when the cotton was picked, the government would send around trucks to pick it up, and that everyone would be given pieces of metal and paper

167

Colonialism deeply influenced the way Africans expressed themselves. These tombs of Nigerian royalty display European-looking figures, complete with Western-style clothes and even walking sticks. (Marc and Evelyne Bernheim from Rapho Guillumette)

that could be exchanged for cloth and beads and all manner of things at Matadi. In time there would even be a store right there in Ndola, where they could use this new money.

The administrator explained that this was necessary to make the work of the government possible, in setting up a hospital, dispensaries, and schools. He also said that he wanted some of the men of Ndola to volunteer their services for work on the roads. He added that those who did not produce cotton, as required, would be locked up or compulsorily put to work with the road gangs; and that if there were not enough

road-work volunteers, they would simply be forced into
service.

Matungi listened to all this courteously, and then asked for
time to consult with the elders. The consultation evidently did
not take long, and he returned to face the administrator and tell
him that he was sorry, but his village wanted nothing to do
with cotton or road work; they preferred simply to live as they
had always lived, without this new money and the trade goods
that it could buy.

The administrator, unwilling to use force so early in the
program, argued his point and appealed to Masoudi, who, as
usual, was standing apart from the others. Masoudi said that
he had tried to tell his relatives about the ways of the white
man, and about all the good things that were being done at
Madadi, but they had not listened. . . .

The administrator left, and nothing much happened for
some months. Presumably he was sounding out other villages
in the district. But eventually, backed up where necessary by the
authority of armed native police imported from the north, all
the recalcitrant chiefs and headmen were deposed, and more
amenable successors appointed. Masoudi was appointed Capi-
ta, or headman, in Matungi's place. Matungi made no
objection, because he knew that it would make little difference
one way or the other, and he was too sensible to argue with
savages armed with guns. The government, with these armed
savages, an animal people from the north who did not even
circumcise, would get their cotton and road workers, but they
would never break the sacred tie between him and his
people.

Masoudi felt much the same way. He knew that the people
would not give him the allegiance that was Matungi's, but that
he would have authority over them in other matters, in support
of which he could demand the assistance of the police. He
recognized that Matungi's position as ritual leader of the
people would remain unaltered. But this was his, Masoudi's,
chance to prove to the villagers that he had been right from the
start; that he did not possess the Evil Eye, that the ways of the

white man were good, if strange; that all of them could own many goats and metal pots and pans, oil lanterns to see by night, and a bicycle to ride from one village to the next along the new road in a quarter of the time it took to walk. He was convinced that he was right, that odd though they might seem, the white men certainly were powerful, and the thing to do was to acquire the same power by copying their ways. He even saw his friends and relatives eventually coming around to liking him again, and speaking to him and his wife. . . .

Masoudi admitted that he felt some gratification in having behind him the power of the police, though he had been refused a policeman of his own such as the big chiefs had. If he had to use force to show his relatives that he was right about the white man, he would do it. They deserved harsh treatment for the way they had behaved toward him. He saw himself as bringing them all multipocketed clothes, shining metal- and enamelware, oil lanterns and bicycles; in return for which all they had to do was to plant a little cotton and do a little work on the road.

Masoudi has long since given up that dream. He still holds to the conviction that many of the white man's ways of living are good, but he no longer believes that they can be transplanted. And he increasingly regrets having abandoned his heritage.

For Masoudi quickly found that he had both more and less authority than he had bargained for. He was efficient at seeing that the cotton was planted and harvested, for the administration sent people to help supervise until the villagers were accustomed to the procedure. He kept notebooks, listing everyone in the village, how much they planted and how much they harvested. He was prepared to take the blame for anyone who failed to produce the minimum amount, and he took such measures as he thought fit to prevent any failure. These measures included fines of chickens or goats, under threat of calling in the police to take the offenders away and put them in boxes. Of course he never intended to call the police. Masoudi was far too mild a man for that. So he was horrified when on one of his periodic visits a new young administrator ordered some villagers beaten for not having kept their plantations in good order. When he protested on their behalf, Masoudi was told that if he disapproved of beatings, he had better keep a sharper eye on the work, and that if the plantations were as far behindhand on the next visit, he would be beaten himself.

In fact the administrator took all sorts of measures of which Masoudi disapproved strongly—such as compelling men to work on the roads and then fining them because they were behind with their work on the plantations. But in these matters he found that he had no authority at all. It was bitter that he should be blamed for these matters by the villagers.
. . .

Masoudi had learned early the futility of questioning the why of the ways of the white man. He just accepted the fact that they did not understand him any more than he understood

The colonial powers created their own chiefs who "ruled" by European warrant and not by traditional authority. (Photoworld, Inc.)

them, and he tried to make the best of his unhappy position. The government considered that he had taken over all Matungi's powers and responsibilities, but from his point of view it was a sacrilege even to consider the possibility, and sheer stupidity to try to put it into practice. Yet if he was going to be fined every time Matungi did something wrong, he would have to do something about it. And this was what worried him. The more he saw of the white man's ways, the more he fell back on his old beliefs, and to take any action against Matungi was in direct contradiction to all those beliefs.

It was not that Masoudi was any the less convinced about the desirability of many of the things the white man had to offer. Their clothes were far superior, even if, as he had been told, they were the real reason why his villagers had to plant that ridiculous cotton which everyone knew ruined the soil. The oil lanterns and bicycle were also good things, and so was the hospital in Matadi, and the traveling doctor who was much better at curing some illnesses than Matungi had ever been. Even the road was a good thing. . . . [But] what Masoudi could never understand was why the white man expected him and the others to change their beliefs, to abandon the ways of the ancestors. Why should it not be possible to continue in the way of the ancestors, the way they *had* to follow if they were not to be condemned to the world of spirits and ghosts after death, and still wear the white man's clothes, grow his cotton, and look after his roads? Did the black man expect the white man to change *his* beliefs, to abandon *his* traditions?

POSTSCRIPT: Masoudi had difficulty enforcing his new authority over the traditional authority of the Chief, Matungi, because he derived his "right" to rule from the Europeans, whereas Matungi derived his right directly from his own people. It was common practice during the colonial period for the Europeans to create their own chiefs who "ruled" by colonial government warrants rather than by traditional authority. Hence, such chiefs were called "warrant chiefs." It was often the most ambitious, upstart members of a community—those without any traditional status—who would ingratiate themselves with the colonialists in hopes of gaining favor and perhaps warrant chief status. When they did gain power, they often used this power in a heavy-handed way, creating conflict within their own communities and especially with traditional leaders.

Ibrahimo Becomes a Christian

❧ INTRODUCTION: Most Africans admit that the Christian missionaries did an enormous amount of good in Africa. They educated the young, nursed the sick, and trained scores of village workers. Speaking of the missionaries in a editorial, the *Reporter Magazine* in Nairobi, Kenya, said: "They have made an impact on the minds of men and women which adds up to a tremendous power for good. . . . For every 'convert' they can add to their list of achievements a dozen craftsmen, skilled in various trades; a score of educated Africans who are now running the affairs of their countries. . . ."

There is no doubt that Christian missionaries brought some of the most beneficial aspects of Western culture to Africa. But they also brought an alien religion that conflicted with traditional African beliefs. The missionaries were single-minded in their goal: they went to the "dark continent" first and foremost to win souls for Christ. If this meant building hospitals, then they built hospitals, but while they healed wounds, they also preached the gospel.

Moreover, the missionaries, as even devout Christians will admit, were extremely narrow in their outlook. They taught that Christianity was the *only* right religion and that all other religious practices must stop. Such teachings confused the Africans, who believed that all religions were good and saw no reason for abandoning their own beliefs in order to adopt some of the good aspects of Christianity.

In the following selection, Ibrahimo, a Congolese boy about 12 years old, becomes a victim of religious conflict. He wants to join the other boys of his age in the all-important ceremony of circumcision, the ritual that marks the passage from boyhood to manhood. Such initiation rites are very common throughout Africa and in other parts of the world; they have been practiced for centuries. Most cultures, in fact, observe some form of initiation into adulthood. In the West, the

174

Jewish bar mitzvah and the Christian confirmation are the most common rites of passage.

Ibrahimo's father was a Christian convert. When he discovered that his son wanted to go through the traditional African ceremony, he notified the local missionary, who put a stop to it. The manner in which this missionary interfered is not typical (although the story is true), but it does indicate the determination of Christian missionaries in Africa to stamp out traditional beliefs.

As you read this selection, bear in mind that the initiation ceremony is the most significant event in a young African's life. His participation makes him a full member of the tribe (now commonly referred to as "ethnic group"). Indeed, it makes him a full human being, for without an ethnic identity, a person is nothing in traditional Africa.[23] ❧

"I do not think my father was a Christian when he married my mother; I know they married in the way of our own people anyway. But he became a Christian before I entered my mother's stomach, and took the name Isaaka. So when I was born and had shown that I had come to this world to stay, he called my Ibrahimo, because it is our custom to name our children after their grandfathers. I do not know what my grandfather's name really was; my father never speaks of him.

"By becoming a Christian my father won a good job as a cook at the Mission. He had to leave because my mother refused to change her ways, and the Mission would not have her there living with him, because they said they were not married. So they returned to Ndola and I was born here and have lived here ever since. There are other Christians at Ndola, but my father has told me that the Mission does not want us to have anything to do with them; they do not believe in the same God. Their leader uses his *baraza* [home] as a church, and has services every Sunday, but we never go; it would be a sin. My father did not like me to play with their children, so at Ndola I have no Christian friends. But I used to have plenty of other friends, and my mother was always very good to us and gave us plenty of good things to eat when we were hungry.

"As I grew older my father said I should not play even with

These young Africans receiving communion from a Catholic priest have been exposed to beliefs that will deeply affect their traditional culture. (Photoworld, Inc.)

my own brothers, and that I should go away to school, to the Mission on the far side of Matadi. My mother did not like this, and there was much fighting and beating. In the end, my mother left my father and while she was away I was taken to school.

"It was a good place, though all the buildings were made of brick and were hot, unlike the houses we built. And we were not allowed to light fires inside at night, to keep us safe and to keep the mosquitoes away. Even if we could have lit them, it would not have done much good, as every wall was broken open with windows, and the smoke would all have escaped. But we learned many things, how to read and write and how to play the strange games of the white man with leather balls. This hurt my feet terribly at first, for we were not allowed to wear shoes, although nearly all of us had them. They said it would spoil the shoes. . . .

"It was difficult to know how to be a Christian, because

Bwana Spence [the missionary] did not like to be asked questions. He read to us from the Big Book and often it did not make sense. When I was still new there I would ask questions, and sometimes he would answer them, but usually he said I did not have to understand, I just had to believe what he said. He got very angry if we asked about all the men in the Big Book who had so many wives, when he taught us that when we were older we should have only one. He said that Bwana Yesu [Jesus] said so. But neither Bwana Yesu nor any of his brothers had any wives, so how could they know? . . .

"There were some things that could not be just because Bwana Spence did not understand. In his teachings he told us to be like brothers to each other, to share everything we had and to help each other. But while there were many of us in one house, sleeping in the same room even though we were from different tribes, he had a house all to himself. He ate three big meals a day while we had two, and his food was much better and much more plentiful. He bought all manner of things at Matadi to eat himself, and we never tasted any of it. He had lots of clothes, and he had many servants to wait on him and do all his work for him. He never asked us into his house, although he would come to ours. In the evenings even if his wife was at the hospital and he was alone, he would not talk to any of us, but just stayed by himself, eating and drinking his tea or coffee. He was never without food, day or night. He must have been very wealthy.

"He had a child too . . . but he would not let her play with any of us or even talk to us. There were some other white children at the Mission but they all lived in the white man's houses, and were taught separately and ate separately and played separately. It was a pity. They could have had a lot of happiness with us.

"Bwana Spence's wife was a proud woman who did not smile. She gave orders, even to men, and got very angry when anyone disobeyed her. She taught the white children, and she worked at the hospital. She always looked as though she was going to be sick, although when I asked her once if she was not well, she said she was perfectly all right. She lied. She was not all right. A relative of mine came to the hospital while I was there because her stomach was full and hurting, but the child would not come. She had been bound with vines and had tried everything she knew to make the child come, but it refused. When Bwana Spence's wife saw her, she told her that the child had not wanted to come because it had been put into the stomach in sin. It could still be saved, she said, if my relative would become a Christian and have a Christian marriage. But my relative was already married, and said she could not be married again. I think the Bwana Spence's wife put a curse on her, because the first part of the child to come out was a hand, and the rest of it was dead. They say that this was one time when Bwana Spence's wife smiled.

We were allowed to go home during the holidays, but I liked it at the school because I had many friends there, and at Ndola the people thought of me as being different, like my father, and they laughed at me. But the longer I stayed at the Mission, the more I was worried. They were doing very good things for us, but they did not seem to like us or want us to be their friends. They were very selfish about their God too, and although they used to ask Him, when we all talked to Him together, to look after us and save our souls and accept us as His children, they never let us stand up and ask for things. They would ask for new motor cars or for money to make roads so that they could travel farther and meet more of our people and make them Christians, but they never let *us* ask for motor cars.

"And once when Bwana Spence's girl child was hot with fever, he made us all ask together for her to be made better, though none of us had even spoken to her. We thought this funny, because she had been hot with fever before, as we all were at times, and it was nothing serious. But we asked for her to be made better, and two days later she was. But that same week a man was brought in who was very ill indeed, and Bwana Spence did not even go to see him, and did not ask God to help him because, he said, the man was not a Christian. We

Mission schools taught more than religion. Here a Dutch priest teaches a student the first notes of the Dutch national anthem. (Photoworld, Inc.)

all thought this was a terrible thing, and we wondered and talked among ourselves about what kind of God this was. We knew we could not ask Bwana Spence, so we asked Amboko. Amboko was almost as cross with us as Bwana Spence would have been, for the man was his relation. I think he was cross because he could not explain it either. I began to wonder if I would be allowed to ask God to help my mother if she became ill, because she is not a Christian. Amboko said no, I would have to ask the ancestors, that they would always listen.

"I had been at the school perhaps two years when

something very bad happened. I was home on vacation and one day Matungi came up to me and took me into the plantation to talk with me. This was a great honor, for Matungi is really our chief, and he is a great and good man. I think I knew what he wanted, though, and I was afraid. It had been three years since the last *nkumbi* initiation festival, and it was time for another. At this festival we boys are taken and we are made into men. It is a very difficult and dangerous thing . . . and we are given the marks on our bodies that make us acceptable to the ancestors. These festivals used to last many months, even a year, but now the Bwana Mkubwa at Matadi does not like it because he says it is evil. They do not know, because they do not understand and are as ignorant about it as little children.

"Matungi told me that it was time for me to enter the *nkumbi,* and to learn the ways of my ancestors. He said that he did not mind me learning to read and write, or even being a Christian, but that it was very wrong for me to forget who I was. He said that only by seeing the *nkumbi* could I make myself fit for the ancestors; by becoming like them, I could become one of them. This was plainly a good thing, and Matungi further showed me that no matter what the Christians said, nobody could deny that I had a father, and he had a father, and his father before him had a father. Nobody could deny that we did have ancestors, and if we had ancestors, how could it be right to neglect and disrespect them when they made life possible for us? I told Matungi that even the Christian teaching said the same thing, and told us that we were to honor our fathers and mothers.

"Matungi was very wise, and I told him that although I was frightened, I *did* want to see the *nkumbi.* He was very pleased, and he gave me a cigarette and told me that I would soon be a real man, and that I would be glad. He also told me not to be frightened, that only children were frightened.

"I ran straight back through the plantation to the village and told my brothers. They were all very surprised, and they congratulated me and said they were happy, because they had been afraid that I would be separated from them and not become a man with them. Now we would all do this dangerous thing together and become men together, and we would all learn the wonderful secrets about our ancestors, and learn how to please them and earn a place beside them in the after-world.

* * *

"Late that night there was a big noise in the village, and I was . . . sorry, because I had wanted it to be a good night—it was the first time I had ever slept with my brothers. I dreamed of all the wonderful times to come, and of all the friends I would have from now on. Early in the morning I hurried out to my mother's plantation, but she was not there. I went home, and she was not there, neither was my father. This was not strange, as everyone goes about his work in the morning, so I went back to the plantation to wait for my mother. She did not come.

"At last, when my stomach was crying for food, my father came, calling my name. I ran up to him and waited for him to speak, but he hit me on the back with his fist and said I had done a terrible thing. He had worked hard to send me to the Mission school, and he had sent me a little money each month so that I could buy things I needed, and now I wanted to throw it all away by seeing the *nkumbi*. He took me back to the house and locked me in, throwing me a little food that had been left over from the morning. I was cold and I could not eat it. I called for my mother, but she did not answer. I didn't know how many days I was kept there; I only remember thinking that I must truly still be a child because I cried so much, but I could not help it.

"What followed is so bad that I try to forget it, and I do not like to talk about it. One morning the Bwana Spence's motor car came and I was put into it and driven away. I still had not seen my mother, and although I saw Matungi and called to him from the window, he just turned away. If I had been a man, I

Chrisianity became firmly established in Africa with the ordination of African priests.
(KLeystone Press Agency, Inc.)

would have jumped out, but I could not. I was sick. I was still being sick when we reached the Mission, and I no longer had the strength to lean out of the window. I was sick all over the back of the car. When Bwana Spence saw this, he was more angry that I had ever seen him. He had me taken away to the hospital, to cure my sickness.

"He came to see me later, and I told him that I wanted to see the *nkumbi* just as my father had seen it, that only in that way could I be a man. I told him all that Matungi had said, and he replied that Matungi was evil, and when he died would go to the fires that never go out. I told him about my brothers, and how they were all glad that I was joining them, and how it was the first time I had really played with them. Bwana Spence asked me if I did not have enough friends at the Mission, and I said yes, but they were not my brothers—I wanted to be friends with *them,* and to see the *nkumbi* with them and share their blood, so that we could all live together as men-brothers, and go to the ancestors together. He told me that there was only one ancestry, and that was Bwana Yesu. I said that could not be, because Bwana Yesu was not married and did not have any children. I also told him that I thought Bwana Yesu was a lie invented to make us go to the white man's afterworld and be his servants there. I do not know what made me say this thing, because I *did* believe in Bwana Yesu; but I said it, and Bwana Spence said that I was also evil, but that it was Matungi's fault and not mine. He said he would ask Bwana Yesu to forgive me, and that he would not let me go home again for any more holidays. I could stay at the Mission and help keep the place clean. He stood at the end of my bed and asked Bwana Yesu to forgive me and to make me a good Christian again; then he left. As soon as he left I asked Bwana Yesu to forgive me and let me see the *nkumbi,* but I knew in my heart that he would listen to Bwana Spence and not me.

"The next day I was no longer sick, but they still would not let me out of the hospital. They said I was not there because I had been sick but for another reason, and I did not understand what they meant. They came in and took hold of me and made me walk into a special house they have where they bring people who are dying, and cut them open. I was very frightened and tried to break away, because I knew I was not dying and they had told me I was not even sick. I thought that Swana Spence was so angry at me for making his car dirty that he was going to kill me. He was there, in the house, and he smiled at me and said not to be frightened, that he had asked Bwana Yesu to stay with me, and that Bwana Yesu had told him how I wanted to be a man like other men, and had made him understand that this was right. At first I thought he meant that I was going to be allowed to return home to the *nkumbi,* but he said no, and told me to lie on the table. Only then did I begin to understand. I fought as hard as I could, but I could not get away. I remember Bwana Spence leaning on my arms, holding me down and smiling. But there was no love in his smile, only hate. Then someone put something over my face. It smelled of vomit and I thought I was being sick again. I felt all my life was being taken away from me, and I was sure I was dying. The last thing I remember is Bwana Spence smiling. And then I died.

"When I woke up, I had no feeling. I knew there was a terrible pain in my body, but my mind was empty, and I just did not care about the pain. All I wanted was to *feel* again, to feel as though I was alive. But I could not. I saw the wife of Bwana Spence standing over me, but when she saw I recognized her, she turned away. I saw other people, but they did not mean anything to me. I heard noises, but I just wanted them to stop because they were empty noises. And then I knew I was dead. I knew it because the pain got worse, and as it got worse it no longer came from my whole body, it came from one place. The place where they had cut me with their knives. I could not see the cut, I could not see the blood, because I was covered with a sheet and I had no strength to move my hands to find what they had done. But I knew, because the pain came from my penis, where they had cut off my skin so that I would never be able to see the *nkumbi*, and would never be able to be a man. I remember crying out loud—not because of the pain, but because of what they had done to me, and I was sick again.

* * *

"I now knew that I had truly died when they brought me into that house of the knife. I knew why Bwana Spence had not wanted to explain things, but tried to make us believe that the words of Bwana Yesu were good words and would help us to be good people. I knew now that his Bwana's kingdom really was in the clouds, although he said it was not, and that it was quite different from ours that is in the earth. I knew that in order to go to Bwana Yesu's kingdom I had to be white and uncircum-

New dreams were planted in the minds of young Africans by European educators.
(Photoworld, Inc.)

cised, and that I could be neither. I also knew that my ancestors would not want me because I had not seen the *nkumbi*.

"I went to see Matungi, and he tried to make me strong. He said that even he did not understand all these matters. He had always thought that Bwana Yesu was a good man, and it was the Bwana Spence who was lying, because he knew of other white men who *were* circumcised. . . ."

"Then I began to hate Bwana Spence because of all his lies, and because of all the unhappiness he had brought to my father and to Matungi and to myself. I felt he was the most evil thing I had ever met, and I asked Matungi to perform a special rite to make both my father and myself clean again in the eyes of our ancestors. But Matungi said he could do it for my father, but that I had not seen the *nkumbi*, and he did not know what he could do for me. He said that the ancestors were able to understand these things, and he would ask them to look after me, and maybe they would talk to him in a dream and tell him what to do.''

"Meanwhile he told me that he thought the best thing was for me to go back to the Mission school and to continue with my learning. They would have to take me back after what they had done, he said. Matungi warned me to have nothing to do with Bwana Spence, not to trust a single white man there, not to believe a word they spoke, and never to join them in their ritual eating and drinking, because this might offend the ancestors even more. 'But,' he said, 'Learn all you can. See for yourself if what Bwana Yesu says is the same thing as what the Bwana Spence says. You have been made one of Bwana Yesu's children by the water ceremony, and after all your father did not see in his dream whether the other children were circumcised or not. He thought they were too young—but maybe the Christians circumcise earlier than we do—and maybe Bwana Spence has an evil spirit in his body that makes him do and say these terrible things. If all that is so, and if you still believe in Bwana Yesu, you may go to his afterworld. You can not come to ours without seeing the *nkumbi*.'

"All this Matungi told me, and my father said that Matungi had spoken well. We would have to accept it that in the afterlife we would be separated forever, for my father had decided to go back to the ways of his ancestors.

"I went back to the school, and I am still there. I have learned a great deal, and I can now read the Big Book myself. But it does not always make sense, and it speaks of many things of which I still know nothing, and it is all about faraway places and about white men that can have nothing to do with me. I try to talk to Bwana Yesu but he does not talk back to me. I stop my ears when I hear Bwana Spence talking, because I do not want to be tricked by his lies. I look in his face and I know he is lying, and that he hates all of us. Even the young children know this and they laugh at him. I once thought of having a child by his daughter, thinking that in this way I might have access to the white man's afterworld, but Matungi told me this would be a very bad thing.

"I do not know what will happen. I am told that the white man is soon going to leave, and then my learning will be useful. But for what? What good is learning if I cannot marry a white girl and if none of our own girl-children will have me? If I cannot in any way make myself clean and acceptable in this world, how can I be fit for life in the afterworld?

"I met some BaNgwana [Muslims] the other day, and they told me that they have a god who will accept me and take me into his afterworld if I do certain things. But they are unclean things. . . . Perhaps I shall have no afterlife, and in that case I can only do what I can with this life. And in this life I shall never believe a white man again. If I follow his ways, it is with my body, not with my heart. In my heart there is only the knowledge that the white man has taken me away from my fathers and brothers for all time, and that he hates me. In that knowledge I can only find strength to hate back."

A Missionary Meets His Match

🌿 INTRODUCTION: Many Africans were not persuaded by the theological arguments of the Christian missionaries. In the following selection, for example, Akunna applies simple logic to decide that his Ibo God, Chukwu, is very much the same and every bit as "good" as Mr. Brown's Christian God. This reading is taken from the novel *Things Fall Apart* by Chinua Achebe, one of Africa's most famous writers.[24] 🌿

Whenever Mr. Brown went to that village he spent long hours with Akunna in his *obi* talking through an interpreter about religion. Neither of them succeeded in converting the other but they learned more about their different beliefs.

"You say that there is one supreme God who made heaven and earth," said Akunna on one of Mr. Brown's visits. "We also believe in Him and call Him Chukwu. He made all the world and the other gods."

"There are no other gods," said Mr. Brown. "Chukwu is the only God and all others are false. You carve a piece of wood—like that one" (he pointed at the rafters from which Akunna's carved *Ikenga* hung), "and you call it a god. But it is still a piece of wood."

"Yes," said Akunna. "It is indeed a piece of wood. The tree from which it came was made by Chukwu, as indeed all minor gods were. But he made them for His messengers so that we could approach Him through them. It is like yourself. You are the head of your church."

"No," protested Mr. Brown. "The head of my church is God Himself."

"I know," said Akunna, "but there must be a head in this world among men. Somebody like yourself must be the head here."

"The head of my church in that sense is in England."

"That is exactly what I am saying. The head of your church is in your country. He has sent you here as his messengers and servants. Or let me take another example, the District Commissioner. He is sent by your king."

"They have a queen," said the interpreter on his own account.

"Your queen sends her messenger, the District Commissioner. He finds that he cannot do the work alone and so he appoints *kotma* to help him. It is the same with God, or Chukwu. He appoints the smaller gods to help Him because His work is too great for one person."

"You should not think of him as a person," said Mr. Brown. "It is because you do so that you imagine He must need

Western technology and Christianity became intermingled and sometimes confused in the minds of many Africans. (Marc and Evelyne Bernheim from Rapho Guillumette)

helpers. And the worst thing about it is that you give all the worship to the false gods you have created."

"That is not so. We make sacrifices to the little gods, but when they fail and there is no one else to turn to we go to Chukwu. It is right to do so. We approach a great man through his servants. But when his servants fail to help us, then we go to the last source of hope. We appear to pay greater attention to the little gods but that is not so. We worry them more because we are afraid to worry their Master. Our fathers knew that Chukwu was the Overlord and that is why many of them gave their children the name Chukwuka—'Chukwu is Supreme.' "

"You said one interesting thing," said Mr. Brown. "You are afraid of Chukwu. In my religion Chukwu is a loving Father and need not be feared by those who do His will."

"But we must fear Him when we are not doing His will," said Akunna. "And who is to tell His will? It is too great to be known."

Anglo-Saxon Destiny

❧ INTRODUCTION: Many of the European colonists had no idea how profoundly they were disrupting the traditional cultures of Africa; they were simply insensitive to the beliefs and customs of other people. Others, however, intentionally tried to destroy African practices, in the conviction that European ways were superior. All of the missionaries and many of the other colonialists felt that they had a sacred duty to bring civilization to "backward" people; it was the "white man's burden" to do so.

The following demonstrates the cultural arrogance of many Europeans during the colonial period. The author, Josiah Strong, an American Congregational minister, felt that Anglo-Saxons (by which he means "the English, the British colonists, and the people of the United States") had a historic mission to bring "civil liberty" and spiritual Christianity to the rest of the world. He presented these ideas in his book *Our Country*, published in 1885.[25] ❧

Every race which has deeply impressed itself on the human family has been the representative of some great idea—one or more—which has given direction to the nation's life and form to its civilization. Among the Egyptians this . . . idea was life, among the Persians it was light, among the Hebrews it was purity, among the Greeks it was beauty, among the Romans it was law. The Anglo-Saxon is the representative of two great ideas, which are closely related. One of them is that of civil liberty. Nearly all of the civil liberty in the world is enjoyed by Anglo-Saxons: the English, the British colonists, and the people of the United States. . . .

The other great idea . . . is that of a pure *spiritual* Christianity. . . . That means that most of the spiritual Christianity in the world is found among Anglo-Saxons and their converts; for this is the great missionary race. . . .

It follows, then, that the Anglo-Saxon, as the great representative of these two ideas, the depository of these two great blessings, sustains peculiar relations to the world's future, is divinely commissioned to be, in a peculiar sense, his brother's keeper. . . .

Another marked characteristic of the Anglo-Saxon is what may be called an instinct or genius for colonizing. His unequaled energy, his indomitable perseverence, and his personal independence made him a pioneer. He excels all others in pushing his way into new countries. It was those in whom this tendency was strongest that came to America, and this inherited tendency had been further developed by the westward sweep of successive generations across the continent. So noticeable has this characterisitc become that English visitors remark it. Charles Dickens once said that the typical

A royal party, consisting of the late King George VI of England, his wife, Queen Elizabeth, and his daughter, Princess Elizabeth (now Queen), inspects the colonies. (Photoworld, Inc.)

American would hesitate to enter heaven unless assured that he could go further west. . . .

It seems to me that God, with infinite wisdom and skill, is training the Anglo-Saxon race for an hour sure to come in the world's future. . . .

Is there room for reasonable doubt that this race, unless devitalized by alcohol and tobacco, is destined to dispossess many weaker races, assimilate others, and mold the remainder, until, in a very true and important sense, it has Anglo-Saxonized mankind? Already "the English language, saturated with Christian ideas, gathering up into itself the best thought of all the ages, is the great agent of Christian civilization throughout the world; at this moment affecting the destinies and molding the character of half the human race." Jacob Grimm, the German philologist, said of his language: "It seems chosen, like its people, to rule in future times in still greater degree in all the corners of the earth." He predicted, indeed, that the language of Shakespeare would eventually become the language of mankind. Is not Tennyson's noble prophecy to find its fulfillment in Anglo-Saxondom's extending its dominion and influence—

> Till the war-drum throbs no longer,
> and the battle-flags are furl'd
>
> In the Parliament of man, the
> Federation of the world.

"Is There Anybody Here?"
and
Martyr

❧ INTRODUCTION: Perhaps the most humiliating aspect of colonialism was the way Europeans treated Africans. It is one thing to lose land and political power, but it is quite another to lose dignity as a person.

"Is There Anybody Here?" illustrates the dehumanizing effects of colonialism in Africa. It was written by Tom Mboya and taken from his book, *Freedom and After*. Until his death by an assassin's bullet in 1969, Mboya was one of the most promising leaders in Africa. He was Kenya's Minister of Finance. [26]

The poem "Martyr" tells the whole story of colonialism in a few lines. The author, David Diop, one of West Africa's best-known poets, was killed in a plane crash in 1960, at the age of thirty-three. [27] ❧

"Is There Anybody Here?"

Working as a sanitary inspector for the Nairobi City Council brought me face to face with racial prejudice in a way I had not known before.

One day in 1951, when one of my European colleagues was away on leave, I was working alone in the food section of the Health Department, testing milk samples. European dairy farmers had to come to us for licenses to bring their milk into Nairobi for sale, and our job was to see that the milk was free of disease and conformed to certain standards. I was in the

194

Delightfully unaware of Queen Elizabeth's photograph, these girls continue to arrange their hair in traditional African styles. (Pictorial Parade, Inc.)

laboratory busy with some tests when a European woman came in with a sample bottle of milk. She looked around for a few moments and did not say anything.

"Good morning, madame," I said.

When I spoke, she turned round and asked, "Is there anybody here?"

I was a bit shocked and angry, but decided her question

was amusing. So I asked, "Is there something wrong with your eyes?"

She was furious and rushed away to find the mayor and the chief sanitary inspector. I had been cheeky and disrespectful, she complained, and the next day she brought a petition she had persuaded other farmers to sign saying they did not want to deal with an African and wanted a European inspector instead. The chief sanitary inspector told the woman she would have to deal with an African if she wanted her license, and the mayor took no action on the petition. He came to me later and said I should not mind these reactions, which were to be expected.

But there were a good many other racial incidents. I was put under a European inspector to gain experience, and the two of us went around Nairobi together several times in the course of our work. I was surprised to find that from time to time he expected me to sit in the car when he went to inspect premises. I refused to do this and we had some heated words. He drove back to City Hall and said we could never work together again.

A number of times I was thrown out of premises I had gone to inspect by Europeans who insisted they wanted a European, not an African, to do the job. The City Council had to prosecute some of them for obstructing African inspectors in the course of their duties. But even inside the department there was discrimination. African inspectors were paid only one fifth of the salary which a European inspector received for doing the same job. African inspectors were told to do their work in khaki uniforms, while the Europeans wore lounge suits. I objected and said either we should all wear uniforms or should all be free to wear what we liked. . . .

Martyr

The White Man killed my father,
My father was proud.
The White Man seduced my mother,

My mother was beautiful.
The White Man burnt my brother
    beneath the noonday sun.
My brother was strong.
His hands red with black blood
The White Man turned to me;
And in the Conqueror's voice said,
"Boy! a chair, a napkin, a drink."

Part IV: The Rise of Nationalism: Freedom Regained

Introduction

The colonial period in most of Africa lasted a relatively short time, from 1885 to about 1960. During that period, Europeans dominated much of the world. Their conquering flags flew in almost every corner of the globe—from the Belgian Congo to the Dutch West Indies, from French Indo-China to Portuguese Guinea, from the British West Indies to India and Burma. It was said, and with justification, that "the sun never sets on the British Empire." The same could have been said of the dominions of other European powers.

The impact of European colonialism on the world's people was enormous. Today, college students in India attend lectures in English; poets in Senegal write in French; judges in Kenya wear British-style wigs; and government documents in Mozambique are written in Portuguese. During the 19th and 20th centuries, Western influence reached almost every culture on earth and pervaded virtually every aspect of life, from medicine and religion to education and sports, from music and language to social customs and eating habits. And, that influence continues to spread today, although the colonial system that launched this Westernization process has come to an end. The sun has set on the colonial period, and most lands that were formerly controlled by European powers are now independent.

Since 1947, more than 80 former colonies have won their freedom. The United Nations, which had 51 members in 1945, has 159 members as of this writing, with most of the new members coming from the so-called developing world, often referred to as the Third World. In fact, the Afro-Asian block in the U.N. today constitutes a majority of the member nations, underscoring the political significance of the rise of nationalism in the Third World. Even more important, the nationalist movements have freed more than half of humankind from colonial subjugation. As Ndabaningi Sithole, an African nationalist from Zimbabwe, has written:

> That 230,000,000 Africans are now free has a significance which it would take a separate volume to explain. At the turn of the present century the African population that will have been born between now and then will be living in freedom and independence. They will walk with their heads held up in full human dignity since Africa for the most part has ceased to breed "unfree" men and women. She now breeds free men and women who no longer have to bow to foreign rulers.
>
> People now live for themselves and not for foreign rulers. They now get education for their own sakes. They can now develop at their own pace without having to be controlled by the temperament of foreign rulers. They are now people. They feel they are people. Men and women of other nationalities and races now regard them as full persons. They now belong to their country. They can now say "Our Country." No amount of money or wealth could have given them this feeling. Only freedom and independence give this priceless feeling.[1]

World War II is usually considered to be the great dividing line between the colonial period and the period of independence, which is still unfolding. This is certainly the case in Africa. Prior to World War II—indeed, until 1950—there were only 3 independent African states: Egypt, Ethiopia, and Liberia. Today there are 51. What happened?

---

[1] Ndabaningi Sithole, *African Nationalism*, New York: Oxford University Press, 1969, p. 3.

FACTORS IN CHANGE

First, African soldiers came home in 1945 after fighting side by side with Europeans throughout the world. They saw their white comrades die as easily as they did (they even saw them defeated in battle by non-European Japanese), and they came to realize that "white superiority" was a myth. At the same time they met black American soldiers who provided them with living examples of non-colonized "Africans."

Secondly, the number of young Africans with a formal education increased dramatically, especially the number studying in European and American universities. The more education they obtained, the more these students became aware of their unequal status under colonial regimes. This was particularly true of students who went abroad. Not only did they study democracy in theory, but they experienced it in life outside the colonies. When they returned to Africa, holding the same Oxford or Cambridge degree as their European rulers, they saw the absurdity of taking orders from "equals" or, worse, from foreigners, and receiving less pay for the same job at that.

Thirdly, the world had changed. The colonial powers of Europe were greatly weakened by the war and had to turn most of their energy to rebuilding their own countries. Thus they were in no position to stem the rising tide of nationalism abroad, although they tried desperately to do so. At the same time, two "new" powers, the Soviet Union and the United States, emerged from the war as world leaders, and neither had much interest in preserving the old colonial system. Moreover, the United Nations, which was formed in 1945, contributed to the anticolonial atmosphere by giving an international forum to nationalist leaders. And, finally, in 1947, India won its hard-fought battle for independence against England, leading the way for the rest of the colonial world. After all, if a power like England could be ousted from India, where it had been entrenched for 200 years, how long could the Europeans last in Africa, where their colonies were barely 60 years old?

INDEPENDENCE: 1950
(Only independent countries are shown.)

*Although technically South Africa gained its independence from England in 1910 and was from that time on no longer a colony, a white minority still controls the country. Therefore, for the Africans, South Africa is still an illegal colonial state.

INDEPENDENCE: 1991

THE CRY FOR UHURU

Thus the stage was set, and the cry for *Uhuru*—freedom—thundered across the African continent. Political parties were organized, mass rallies were held, flags were waved, and everywhere the message was the same: "Europeans, Go Home!" In the vanguard of the attack was the British colony of the Gold Coast. In 1957, led by the great nationalist Kwame Nkrumah, the Gold Coast—today known as Ghana—became the first tropical African state to win independence.

Once Ghana broke loose, the rest of the colonial structure collapsed. In 1958, President de Gaulle of France invited the French colonies of Africa to decide by vote whether to remain in the French community or to become independent. Only one country, Guinea, chose the latter course. (The others presumably feared that independence would cut their economic ties to France.) Within two weeks the French had left Guinea, but not without showing their spite by ripping out telephones and light fixtures and destroying government documents. These final acts, however, were as futile as they were childish, for by 1960 11 more French colonies had followed Guinea's lead. Belgian and English colonies likewise gained their independence during the early 1960's, and by 1975 most of Africa was free. (See "Independence Ledger," on p. 272)

In most cases, Africans did not have to resort to violence to win their freedom, with the major exceptions being those colonies held by Portugal and those with large white settler communities. In the Portuguese colonies of Angola, Guinea-Bissau, and Mozambique, it took more than a decade of guerrilla warfare to win independence. Similarly, it took the Mau Mau revolt to unsettle the white planters in Kenya, and a guerrilla war and international economic sanctions to oust the white minority government of Southern Rhodesia. South Africa is still controlled by a white minority, and Namibia is controlled by South Africa, so the struggle for African independence goes on.

THE EUROPEAN LEGACY

An interesting aspect of the nationalist movement in Africa, and elsewhere in the world as well, is that it was made possible by the colonizers themselves: the Europeans. The very concept of a "nation" or "nation-state" is Western. It was Europeans who first established the pattern of bringing small, diverse groups of people together to form a larger unit to which all members paid their allegiance. Certainly such *nations* as the Ivory Coast, Nigeria, the Congo, and Uganda did not exist before the Europeans created them.

Moreover, the very nature of European colonialism gave rise to nationalist activities. Racial discrimination and economic exploitation led to the creation of African social clubs and labor unions, which in time served as the foundation of political parties. At the same time, Western education, both in Africa and abroad, taught theories of political liberty, and the Europeans themselves, by their presence in Africa, gave examples of political organization. In a very real sense, then, African nationalism grew out of the soil of colonialism. The Europeans laid the groundwork for the eventual downfall of their own regimes.

Some scholars point out, however, that nations existed in Africa before the coming of the Europeans, and long before the onset of colonialism in 1885. They point to the medieval Sudanic kingdoms of Ghana, Mali, and Songhay, and to the "nations" of the Ashanti, Ewe, Yoruba, Zulu, Buganda, and Kikuyu. These latter groups, although formerly (and sometimes disparagingly) called tribes, are certainly large enough in number and complex enough in organization to be called "nations" according to most definitions.

But whether we believe that Europeans brought nationalism to Africa or that it had existed there before their coming, one thing is certain: European colonialism created a new type of nationalism in Africa. First of all, the twentieth-century nationalists who grew up under colonialism were not traditional leaders. They were a new breed: young, Western-educated, urbanized, and scientific in outlook.

Secondly, the nations themselves—that is, their geographic boundaries—were drawn by Europeans during the "scramble" for Africa. These "nations" had never existed before. Indeed, the Europeans paid so little attention to the natural political groupings that already existed in Africa that they sometimes drew national boundaries through the middle of ethnic territories. Today, for example, the Somalis live in Kenya and Ethiopia as well as in their own country, Somalia, and the Ewe are split between Ghana and Togo. Such division of natural groups leads to border disputes. Imagine what would happen if Mexico's border were suddenly extended as far north as Los Angeles!

Not only did the Europeans divide natural groupings when they formed their African colonies, they also forced into a single political unit ethnic groups that had nothing in common: neither language, custom, religion, nor history. Some African nations have as many as a hundred distinct ethnic groups within their borders.

The European legacy, then, is a mixed blessing. It left large units in the place of smaller ones, thereby creating African nations that could exist on a par with other nations of the world. But at the same time, it left problems that will take a long time to solve.

The Parable of the Eagle

❧ INTRODUCTION: Although the great thrust for independence came after World War II, there were occasional protests and strikes as early as the 1920's and 1930's. These early stirrings, however, were usually handled by discussion and compromises, conducted by traditional chiefs and urbanized lawyers and teachers. Without a mass movement, these African leaders were forced to bargain with the Europeans, and they got very little.

One of the most prominent nationalists of that time was James Aggrey, a college principal from the Gold Coast (Ghana) and a boyhood hero of Kwame Nkrumah. Aggrey had spent several years as a student and teacher in North Carolina and was instrumental in convincing Nkrumah to study in the United States. In keeping with the spirit of the times, Aggrey was a moderate, and he is best known for his statement that harmony on the piano requires both black and white keys.[28] ❧

A certain man went through a forest seeking any bird of interest he might find. He caught a young eagle, brought it home and put it among his fowls and ducks and turkeys, and gave it chickens' food to eat even though it was an eagle, the king of birds.

Five years later a naturalist came to see him and, after passing through his garden, said: "That bird is an eagle, not a chicken."

"Yes, said its owner, "but I have trained it to be a chicken. It is no longer an eagle, it is a chicken, even though it measures fifteen feet from tip to tip of its wings."

"No," said the naturalist, "it is an eagle still: it has the heart of an eagle, and I will make it soar high up to the heavens."

Shouts—and shots—rang out across Africa in celebration of independence. (Wide World Photos)

"No," said the owner, "it is a chicken, and it will never fly."

They agreed to test it. The naturalist picked up the eagle, held it up, and said with great intensity: "Eagle, thou art an eagle; thou dost belong to the sky and not to this earth; stretch forth thy wings and fly."

The eagle turned this way and that, and then, looking down, saw the chickens eating their food, and down he jumped.

The owner said: "I told you it was a chicken."

"No," said the naturalist, "it is an eagle. Give it another chance tomorrow."

So the next day he took it to the top of the house and said: "Eagle, thou art an eagle; stretch forth thy wings and fly." But again the eagle, seeing the chickens feeding, jumped down and fed with them.

Then the owner said: "I told you it was a chicken."

"No," asserted the naturalist. "It is an eagle, and it still has the heart of an eagle; only give it one more chance, and I will make it fly tomorrow."

The next morning he rose early and took the eagle outside the city, away from the houses, to the foot of a high mountain. The sun was just rising, gilding the top of the mountain with gold, and every crag was glistening in the joy of that beautiful morning.

He picked up the eagle and said to it: "Eagle, thou art an eagle; thou dost belong to the sky and not to this earth; stretch forth thy wings and fly!"

The eagle looked around and trembled as if new life were coming to it; but it did not fly. The naturalist then made it look straight at the sun. Suddenly it stretched out its wings and, with the screech of an eagle, it mounted higher and higher and never returned. It was an eagle, though it had been kept and tamed as a chicken!

My people of Africa, we were created in the image of God, but men have made us think that we are chickens, and we still think we are; but we are eagles. Stretch forth your wings and fly! Don't be content with the food of chickens!

The New Politics

❧ INTRODUCTION: At the base of the colonial philosophy was the myth that European culture was superior to African culture, that whites were "civilized" and "moral" while blacks were "backward" and "savage." It follows, of course, that the "clean" white people should not mix with the "dirty" black people: hence the practice of racial segregation.

Another part of this myth, perhaps less cruel but no less insidious, was the idea that "colored people" were children and needed guidance. Thus it became the "white man's burden" to help these poor, unfortunate people to grow up. Nothing was more infuriating to the Africans than this patronizing attitude. And when the Europeans used this myth to obstruct African independence, counseling the Africans to "go slow," "wait until you are ready" (by which they meant wait 50 or 100 years), the Africans answered with a resounding "Freedom Now!"

To destroy Africans' beliefs in the white myths was one thing, but to change the politics of the continent was quite another.

The colonial regimes controlled all the centers of power: the government, the army, the schools, and most important, the jobs. Africans' attempts to bargain with the Europeans won little more than token concessions. It became obvious that a more powerful force was needed to bring real change. That new force was mass movements. As Kwame Nkrumah pointed out: "A middle-class elite, without the battering ram of the illiterate masses, can never hope to smash the forces of colonialism. Such a thing can be achieved only by a united people organized in a disciplined political party and led by that party."

Nkrumah led the way in black Africa by organizing such a party in Ghana. On June 12, 1949, in Accra, he announced before 60,000 cheering people the creation of the Convention People's Party (CPP). The motto of the party was simple and dramatic: "Self-government

NOW!'' The program of the party, Nkrumah said, would be based on "positive action," by which he meant nonviolent protest similar to the passive resistance practiced by Mahatma Gandhi in India. According to the theory of this program, if the colonial government were to wake up one morning to find the shops closed, the busses stalled, and the offices empty, it might get the idea that it had no country to govern and therefore depart. The theory was tried out and proved to work. On March 6, 1957, after several strikes but without a bloody confrontation, Ghana became the first independent nation in black Africa, and Nkrumah became prime minister.

It took a remarkable man to lead such a mass movement and Kwame Nkrumah was just that. Born in 1909, the son of a poor goldsmith, he worked his way through school and college in Ghana and, with the financial help of an uncle, set sail for the United States in 1935. Four years later he was graduated from Lincoln University, in Pennsylvania, with a Bachelor's degree in economics and sociology. He then studied theology at Lincoln, earned graduate degrees in education and philosophy from the University of Pennsylvania, and eventually returned to Lincoln to teach political science. In 1945 he left for London to complete work on his doctorate and to study law.

Life was not easy for Nkrumah during the years in the United States. He was poor (and black), and to support himself he worked in a soap factory, sold fish on Harlem streets, and washed dishes on ships. Despite these hardships, however, he left the United Sates after 10 years with a sense of hope. Sailing out of New York Harbor, he looked at the Statue of Liberty and said, "I shall never rest until I have carried your message to Africa."

The following selection describes how Nkrumah carried that message to the masses of Ghana, transforming them into a "battering ram" of political power. The author is Richard Wright, the renowned black American writer, who went to Ghana in 1953 to see for himself what Nkrumah was accomplishing.[29] ❧

. . . Next morning a phone call came from the Prime Minister's office; I was told that at four o'clock I'd be picked up by the Prime Minister's car and that I'd see "something."

And at four o'clock a sleek car entered the driveway. A uniformed chauffeur stepped out and saluted me; I climbed into the back seat. As we went through the city black faces jerked around, recognizing the car. We came to the Prime Minister's residence and pulled into a driveway. I got out and

Kwame Nkrumah, African nationalist hero, waves to a cheering crowd of his fellow countrymen gathered in Accra to celebrate the end of the Gold Coast colony and the birth of the independent state of Ghana. Under Nkrumah's leadership, Ghana won its freedom on March 6, 1957, paving the way for other black African states. (United Press)

young black faces smiled at me. A few policmen hovered in the background. I was led forward into a red, two-story brick dwelling that looked remarkably like a colonial mansion in Georgia or Mississippi. I followed my guide upstairs, down a hallway, and into a living room.

The Prime Minister, dressed in a smock, was standing in the middle of the floor.

"Welcome!" he said.

"I'm glad to see you and your people," I told him.

"How are you?"

"Fine, but panting to see your party and your comrades."

He laughed. He presented me to a series of his friends whose strange names I did not recall, then we sat down.

"I want to take you on a quick tour of the city," he told me.

"I'm truly honored."

"Nothing has been prepared. I want you to see how these people respond to our appeals—"

"What's going to happen in July?" I asked, referring to the coming meeting of the Legislative Assembly.

The Prime Minister threw back his head and laughed. I got used, in time, to that African laughter. It was not caused by mirth; it was a way of indicating that, though they were not going to take you into their confidence, their attitude was not based upon anything hostile.

"You are direct," he said.

"Why not?" I asked.

"You'll have to wait and see," he told me. . . .

His colleagues drew him into a discussion that was conducted in tribal language; when it was over, he announced:

"Let's go!"

His personal bodyguard stood at attention; it was composed of hand-picked militants and faithfuls of the Convention People's Party. He led the way and I followed down into the street where his motorcycle escort, dressed in scarlet, stood lined up near their machines. The Prime Minister waved his hand to signal that all was ready. The motorcyclists raced their engines to a deafening roar; then they pulled slowly into the street, leading the way. The Prime Minister's car, with the Prime Minister seated on my right, followed.

The sun was still shining as we moved slowly forward. The drone of the motorcycles attracted the attention of people on both sides of the street and, spontaneously, men, women, and children abandoned what they were doing and fronted the car. Others rushed pellmell out of shacks, their faces breaking into wide, glad smiles, and, lifting their hands upward with their elbows at the level of their hips, palms fronting forward . . . they shouted a greeting to the Prime Minister in a tone of voice compounded of passion, exhortation and contained joy:

"Free—dooom! Free—dooom!"

Ahead of the car the sides of the streets turned black with faces. We reached a wide roadway and the crowds swirled, shouting:

"Free—dooom! Free—doom!"

"Kwame! Kwame!" They shouted his name.

"Fight! Fight!"

"Akwaba! Akwaba!" ("Welcome! Welcome!")

The road turned into a black river of eager, hopeful, glad faces whose trust tugged at the heart. The crowds grew thicker. The shouting sounded like a cataract. The Prime Minister, smiling, laughing, lifted his right hand as he returned their salute.

The road led into a slum area, and the Prime Minister turned to me and said:

"This is James Town. I want you to see this too. . . . I want you to see all we have, the good and the bad."

The narrow streets filled quickly and the car plowed slowly through . . . crowds of men, women, and children who chanted:

"Free—doooom!"

Many of the women waved their hands in that strange, quivering gesture of welcome which seemed to be common to the entire Gold Coast; it consisted of lifting the hand, but, instead of waving the hand as one did in the West, one held the arm still and shook the palm of the hand nervously and tremblingly from side to side, making the fingers vibrate.

"Free—doooom!"

My mind flew back to the many conversations that I'd had in Chicago, New York, London, Paris, Rome, Buenos Aires about freedom . . . and I could hear again in my memory the tersely deprecating question shot at me across a dinner table: *Freedom? What do you mean, freedom?*

But here in Africa "freedom" was more than a word; an African had no doubts about the meaning of the word "freedom." It meant the right to public assembly, the right to physical movement, the right to make known his views, the right to elect men of his choice to public office, and the right to recall them if they failed in their promises. At a time when the Western world grew embarrassed at the sound of the word "freedom," these people knew that it meant the right to shape their own destiny as they wished. Of that they had no doubt, and no threats could intimidate them about it; they might be cowed by guns and planes, but they'd not change their minds about the concrete nature of the freedom that they wanted and were willing to die for. . . .

The crowds, milling in and out of the space between the motorcycles and the Prime Minister's car, chanted:

"Free—dooooom!"

The passionate loyalty of this shouting crowd had put this man in power, had given him the right to speak for them, to execute the mandate of national liberation that they had placed in his hands; and, because he'd said he'd try, they'd galvanized into a whole that was 4,000,000 strong, demanding an end to their centuries-old thralldom. Though still mainly tribal, though 90 per cent illiterate, they wanted to be free of an alien flag, wanted the sovereignty of their own will in their own land. And they had melted their tribal differences into an instrument to form a bridge between tribalism and twentieth-century forms of political mass organization. The women who danced and shouted were washerwomen, cooks, housewives, etc.

"Free—dooom! Free—dooom!" rang deafeningly in my ears.

"They believe in you," I said to the Prime Minister.

"Four years ago a demonstration like this was impossible," he told me. "These were a cowed and frightened people. Under the British it would have been unheard of for people to sing and shout and dance like this. . . . We changed all that. When I came from London in 1948, the mood of these people was terrible. They trusted nothing and nobody. They'd been browbeaten so long by both the black leaders and the British that they were afraid to act."

* * *

Political rallies, some involving thousands of people, helped to organize the African masses, whose force finally turned the tide in favor of independence after World War II. (Central Press)

We came at last to a block of cement houses; from windows and doorways black faces shouted and called:

"Kwame! Kwame!"

"Free—doom! Free—doom!"

The car stopped and the Prime Minister got out; I followed him.

"What is this?" I asked him.

"This is a meeting of the Women's Division of the party," he told me.

We entered a concrete compound and sat as the meeting, dedicated to reorganization and installment of new officers, got under way. A tall black women led a chant:

"Forward ever, backward never . . ."

There was a relaxed, genial atmosphere; now and then an easy laugh floated over the crowd. The men, clad in their native togas, sat in the rear, rising occasionally to aid in making seating arrangements. In front sat about two hundred women also clad in their native clothes and, for this ceremony, they wore an enormous amount of gold in their ears, around their necks, on their arms and fingers . . .

A psalm was sung in English. Next, an African of the Christian persuasion stepped forward and, in English, led the group in prayer. Then came a pagan chief with his umbrella, his staff, his "linguist," and proceeded to pour a libation of corn wine to the dead ancestors. The two religions nestled snugly, cheek by jowl, and the setting sun shone as calmly as usual; there was not a tremor in the universe. . . . After he emptied the bowl by dribbling the corn wine upon the ground, the chief had the bowl filled again and he passed it around to each person nearby and they took three sips. (Three is the lucky number among many Africans of the Gold Coast.)

A series of speakers rose, both men and women, and, in a mixture of English and tribal tongues, exhorted the women to give all their support to the Leader, to the Convention People's Party, and to the struggle for national liberation. To this . . . was added still another ingredient; a woman rose and proclaimed: "I'm Mrs. Nkrumah!"

A howl of laughter rose from the women. Puzzled, I looked at the Prime Minister; he grinned at me, and said:

"It's a joke."

"I *am* Mrs. Nkrumah!" the woman said in a voice that sought to still all doubts.

The Prime Minister rose and, sweeping his arms to include all the women, said:

"You are *all* my brides!"

The women laughed and clapped. Nkrumah, of course, was a bachelor.

"I have to say that to them," he whispered to me as he sat again. "Now, tell me, do you understand what you are looking at?"

"You have fused tribalism with modern politics," I said.

"That's exactly it," he said. "Nobody wanted to touch these people. The missionaries would go just so far and no farther toward them. One can only organize them by going where they are, living with them, eating with them, sharing their lives. We are making a special drive to enlist women in the party; they have been left out of our national life long enough. In the words of Lenin, I've asked the cooks to come out of their kitchens and learn how to rule."

The new women officials to be installed were called to come forward and stand fronting the Prime Minister. A short statement of aims and duties was read to them and, at the end, each women was asked to raise her right hand and repeat the following oath (I'm paraphrasing this from memory):

"I pledge with all my life my support to the Convention People's Party, and to my leader, Kwame Nkrumah; I swear to follow my Leader's guidance, to execute faithfully his commands, to resist with all my power all imperialist attempts to disrupt our ranks, to strive with all of my heart to rebuild our lost nation, Ghana, so help me God! . . .

POSTSCRIPT: In 1966, less than 10 years after leading Ghana to independence, Kwame Nkrumah was overthrown in a military coup, illustrating dramatically a lesson that many nationalist leaders were to learn, namely, it is much easier to give speeches calling for freedom than to create the political and economic system that will make freedom meaningful. Nkrumah lived in exile in Guinea until his death on April 27, 1972; his body was returned to Ghana and buried in his home village of Nkroful.

The Congo Wins Freedom

❧ INTRODUCTION: At the peak of the independence movement, Patrice Lumumba held a place in the hearts of Africans equal to that of Kwame Nkrumah. On June 30, 1960, at age 35, Lumumba became the first prime minister of the independent Congo. Only a few months later, in early 1961, he was abducted and killed by political enemies who were said to be supported by the Belgians, former rulers of the Congo. Although his career was brief, Lumumba's life and death have come to symbolize the experience of the Congo: the victory over the Belgians and the bloody conflicts that have riddled the Congo since then. (The Congo changed its name to Zaire in 1971.)

Unlike the British and the French, the Belgians did not include many Africans in the colonial government, or permit the formation of political parties. As a result, the Congolese were not well trained for administering their country after independence; nor were they united, as other countries were, by a powerful independence party. The result was chaos, created by internal dissention.

The roots of the Congo's difficult beginning as an independent nation can be found in the colonial past. As we have seen, the Belgians took a highly paternalistic attitude toward "their" Africans. They treated them like children, which meant they took care of their simple immediate needs but totally neglected their long-range requirements. For example, the Congolese had better medical care than most Africans, but they had no doctors of their own; they had better housing, but no engineers; they had highly developed industry, but no technicians. In 1960 about 75 per cent of the Congolese children were enrolled in school, but there were only 12 African college graduates in the whole country. The foundation for building a nation, then, was weak, but the desire for freedom—the refusal to be treated like children—was as strong in the Congo as everywhere else in Africa.

In the following selection, Patrice Lumumba, speaking at

Independence Day ceremonies attended by the King of Belgium, recalls some of the injustices the Congolese suffered under Belgian rule and outlines his program for the future.[30] ❧

Your Majesty,
Excellencies, Ladies and Gentlemen,
Congolese men and women,
fighters for independence who today are victorious,
I salute you in the name of the Congolese government.

I ask of you all, my friends who have ceaselessly struggled at our side, that this 30th of June, 1960, may be preserved as an illustrious date etched indelibly in your hearts, a date whose meaning you will teach proudly to your children, so that they in turn may pass on to their children and to their grandchildren the glorious story of our struggle for liberty.

For if independence of the Congo is today proclaimed in agreement with Belgium, a friendly nation with whom we are on equal footing, yet no Congolese worthy of the name can ever forget that it has been by struggle that this independence has been gained, a continuous and prolonged struggle, an ardent and idealistic struggle, a struggle in which we have spared neither our strength nor our privations, neither our suffering nor our blood.

Of this struggle, one of tears, fire, and blood, we are proud to the very depths of our being, for it was a noble and just struggle, absolutely necessary in order to bring to an end the humiliating slavery which had been imposed upon us by force.

This was our fate during eighty years of colonial rule; our wounds are still too fresh and painful for us to be able to erase them from our memories.

We have known the backbreaking work exacted from us in exchange for salaries which permitted us neither to eat enough to satisfy our hunger, nor to dress and lodge ourselves decently, nor to raise our children as the beloved creatures that they are.

We have known the mockery, the insults, the blows

submitted to morning, noon and night because we were "*negres.*" Who will forget that to a Negro one used the familiar term of address, not, certainly, as to a friend, but because the more dignified forms were reserved for whites alone?

We have known the law was never the same, whether dealing with a white or a Negro; that it was accommodating for the one, cruel and inhuman to the other.

We have known the atrocious suffering of those who were imprisoned for political opinion or religious beliefs: exiles in their own country, their fate was truly worse than death itself.

Patrice Lumumba, nationalist leader and first prime minister of the independent Congo, is carried through the streets of Leopoldville on his return from Belgium only a few months before independence on June 30, 1960. The signs say "Long Live the Unity of the Congo" and "Long live the Nationalist Congolese Movement (M.N.C.)," the independence party organized by Lumumba. (Wide World Photos)

We have known that in the cities there were magnificent houses for the whites and crumbling hovels for the Negroes, that a Negro was not admitted to movie theaters or restaurants, that he was not allowed to enter so-called "European" stores, that when the Negro traveled, it was on the lowest level of a boat, at the feet of the white man in his deluxe cabin.

And, finally, who will forget the hangings or the firing squads where so many of our brothers perished, or the cells into which were brutally thrown those who escaped the soldiers' bullets—the soldiers whom the colonialists made the instruments of their domination?

From all this, my brothers, have we deeply suffered.

But all this, however, we who by the vote of your elected representatives are directed to guide our beloved country, we who have suffered in our bodies and in our hearts from colonialist oppression, we it is who tell you—all this is henceforth ended.

The Republic of the Congo has been proclaimed, and our beloved country is now in the hands of its own children.

Together, my brothers, we are going to start a new struggle, a sublime struggle, which will lead our country to peace, prosperity and greatness.

Together we are going to establish social justice and ensure for each man just remuneration for his work.

We are going to show the world what the black man can do when he works in freedom, and we are going to make the Congo the hub of all Africa.

We are going to be vigilant that the lands of our nation truly profit our nation's children.

We are going to re-examine all former laws, and make new ones which will be just and noble.

We are going to put an end to suppression of free thought and make it possible for all citizens fully to enjoy the fundamental liberties set down in the declaration of the Rights of Man.

We are going to succeed in suppressing all discrimination —no matter what it may be—and give to each individual the just place to which his human dignity, his work, and his devotion to his country entitle him.

We shall cause to reign, not the peace of guns and bayonets, but the peace of hearts and good will.

And for all this, dear compatriots, rest assured that we shall be able to count upon not only our own enormous forces and immense riches, but also upon the assistance of numerous foreign countries whose collaboration we shall accept only as long as it is honest and does not seek to impose upon us any political system, whatever it may be.

In this domain, even Belgium, who, finally understanding the sense and direction of history, has no longer attempted to oppose our independence, is ready to accord us its aid and friendship, and a treaty to this effect has just been signed between us as two equal and independent countries. This cooperation, I am sure, will prove profitable for both countries. For our part, even while remaining vigilant, we shall know how to respect commitments freely consented to.

Thus, in domestic as well as in foreign affairs, the new Congo which my government is going to create will be a rich country, a free and prosperous one. But in order that we may arrive at this goal without delay, I ask you all, legislators and Congolese citizens, to help me with all your power.

I ask you all to forget tribal quarrels which drain our energies and risk making us an object of scorn among other nations.

I ask the parliamentary minority to help my government by constructive opposition and to remain strictly within legal and democratic bounds.

I ask you all not to demand from one day to the next unconsidered raises in salary before I have had the time to set in motion an over-all plan through which I hope to assure the prosperity of the nation.

I ask you all not to shrink from any sacrifice in order to assure the success of our magnificent enterprises.

I ask you all, finally, to respect unconditionally the life and the property of your fellow citizens and of the foreigners established in our country. If the behavior of these foreigners leaves something to be desired, our justice will be prompt in expelling them from the territory of the Republic; if, on the other hand, their conduct is satisfactory, they must be left in peace, for they also are working for the prosperity of our country.

And so, my brothers in race, my brothers in conflict, my compatriots, this is what I wanted to tell you in the name of the government, on this magnificent day of our complete and sovereign Independence.

Our government—strong, national, popular—will be the salvation of this country.

Homage to the Champions of National Liberty!

Long Live Independent and Sovereign Congo!

The African Outlook

❧ INTRODUCTION: Nationalism not only brought political freedom to Africa; it created a new pride in African culture. For centuries the Western world had looked down on African culture as "backward" and "uncivilized," and for almost one hundred years European educators in Africa had taught their students that "true" culture was Western.

Africans never really believed this propaganda, but, faced with the dominance of European governments and the power of Western technology, they found little opportunity to assert their own characters. With the rise of nationalism came renewed faith in the African way of life, a new self-confidence about African culture that is best described as *cultural* nationalism. In some ways, this new awareness preceded the political movements and made them possible.

The following selection expresses many of the ideas that emerged during the African cultural revival. Notice that Western culture is no longer the yardstick of achievement; in particular, technological development is superseded as the criterion of success by human relationships (a particularly relevant idea in the age of the bomb and environmental pollution). As an African popular song puts it:

> Those who are blessed with the power
> And the soaring swiftness of the eagle
> And have flown before,
> Let them go,
> I will travel slowly,
> And I too will arrive.

The author of this selection, Dunduzu Kalui Chisiza, was a nationalist leader in Malawi during the 1950's. He was arrested with other leaders in 1959 and upon his release organized the Malawi Congress Party. He was Parliamentary Secretary to the Nyasaland

(Malawi) Ministry of Finance when he was killed in an automobile accident in 1962 at age 32.[31] ⁊

Different as colonial and free Africa may appear to be in temper, in immediate objectives, and in some of the problems which they face, they have one thing in common, and that is their determination to preserve the substance of the African outlook. It is true that there is no uniform outlook. But it is possible to single out certain features which are always present

The African outlook is expressed through art, music, and crafts. The Artists' Center in Oshogbo, Nigeria, provides work and gallery space for gifted African artists. (Marc and Evelyne Bernheim from Rapho Guillumette)

in almost every African community.

Unlike Easterners, who are given to meditation, or Westerners, who have an inquisitive turn of mind, we of Africa, belonging neither to the East nor to the West, are fundamentally observers, penetrating observers, relying more on intuition than on the process of reasoning. We excel in neither mysticism nor in science and technology, but in the field of human relations. This is where we can set an example for the rest of the world . . .

There is a tendency in the West, whether the Westerners themselves know it or not, for people to assume that man lives to work. We believe that man works to live. This view of life gives rise to our high preference for leisure. With us, life has meant the pursuit of happiness rather than the pursuit of beauty or truth. We pursue happiness by rejecting isolationism, individualism, negative emotions, and tensions, on the one hand; and by laying emphasis on a communal way of life, by encouraging positive emotions and habitual relaxation, and by restraining our desires, on the other. We live our lives in the present. To us the past is neither a source of pride nor a cause of bitterness. The "hereafter," we realize, must be given thought, but we fail to revel in its mysteries . . .

In Africa, we believe in strong family relations. We have been urged by well-meaning foreigners to break these ties for one reason or another. No advice could be more dangerous to the fabric of our society. Charity begins at home. So does the love of our fellow human beings. By loving our parents, our brothers, our sisters, cousins, aunts, uncles, nephews, and nieces, and by regarding them as members of our families, we cultivate the habit of loving lavishly, of exuding human warmth, of compassion, and of giving and helping. But I believe that, once so conditioned, one behaves in this way, not only to one's family, but also to the clan, the tribe, the nation, and to humanity as a whole.

If independent African states succeed in subordinating national loyalties to international loyalty they will do so because they have a solid foundation of lesser loyalties. To foster internationalism among people who are steeped in individualism is to attempt to build a pyramid upside down. It cannot stand, it has no base and will topple over. How can a person who has no real affection for his brothers or sisters have any love for a poor Congolese or Chinese peasant? When we talk about international peace, understanding, and good will, we are actually talking about universal love. But this does not grow from nothing; its root is family love, without which it cannot grow. The unification of mankind ultimately depends on the cultivation of family love. It would seem, therefore, that in this respect, we in Africa have started toward that noble goal from the right end.

* * *

In human relations, we like to slur over "I" and "mine" and to lay emphasis instead on "we" and "ours." Put differently, this means the suppression of individuals. Ours is a society where if you found seven men, and one woman among them, you might never know, unless told, whose wife she was. There just isn't that forwardness in us to indicate our "personal" ownership of anything. If I happen to have some head of cattle, a car, a house, a daughter, a fishing net, or a farm, it is "our" net, it is my house just as much as it is my brother's, my father's, my cousin's, my uncle's, or my friend's house. Individualism is foreign to us, and we are horrified at its sight. We are by nature extroverts.

Love for communal activities is another feature of our outlook. Look at any African game or pastime and you notice right away that its performance calls for more than one person. Our dances are party dances demanding drummers, singers, and dancers. Game hunting is done in parties. (Even those Africans who own guns cannot abandon the habit of taking some friends along with them when going out for a hunt!) The telling of fables and stories with us calls for a group of boys and girls, not just one or two. Draw-net fishing is done by a group of people. Fishing with hooks is done also in canoe parties, each canoe taking at least two people. The preparation of fields, the weeding, the sowing of seeds, the harvesting, the pounding of food—all these activities are done in parties of either men or women. Even looking after cattle is not a one-man affair. A boy might start out alone from his cattle kraal but he is sure to take his cattle to where his fellow herdsmen are. Beer drinking is not only a group affair but it often means also drinking from the same pot and from the same drinking stick. Above all, to see Africans mourn the death of someone is to believe that few things are done individually here.

Such an outlook can only emanate from genuine love for each other—an unconscious love which has existed in our society since time immemorial. Here is that selfless love which all the prophets of God have preached. It isn't something that has just been inculcated into us nor anything that has been imported from without us; it is something springing from within us. Instead of foreign missionaries teaching Africans how to love each other, they would do well to sit back and observe with amazement that the very relationship they would like to bring about is already existing in the selfless love manifested in the African way of life.

We are also famous for our sense of humor and dislike for melancholy. Gloom on the face of an African is a sure sign that the wearer of that expression has been to a school of some kind where he might have got it into his head that joy and melancholy can be bed-fellows in his heart. Otherwise our conception of life precludes as far as possible the accommodation of dejection. An African will not hesitate to leave a job if he sees that he does not get a kick out of it . . .

The mainstay of our life is humor. So characteristic of Africa is this that most foreigners know this continent as "The Land of Laughter." Of course, laughter relieves tension. People who laugh easily are relaxed persons and possess one of the most prized qualities in this wearisome world.

Our society abhors malice, revenge, and hate, with the result that we are relatively free from these cankers. Were we disposed to avenge the wrongs that have been meted out to us by foreigners down through the ages, the course of human events would have taken a different turn altogether. Were we addicts of hate, the Gospel of Jesus would have been defeated on the shores of the seas that border this troubled continent. Were we to harbor malice, the African empires that flourished —like those of Monomotapa, Songhai, Mali, and Ghana— would have extended beyond the confines of Africa to the detriment of the human race. But God spared us all that. As a result we tolerate on our soil even neurotic crowds of foreigners who could not be tolerated in their own countries; we waste love on those who are inveterately selfish, individualistic, and ungrateful. Above all, we do not look forward to planning nefarious schemes against any race.

We have a reputation for taking delight in generosity, kindness, and forgiveness. It has been said with great truth by foreigners that few Africans will ever get rich because we tend to be too generous. Well, we do not want to be rich at the cost of being mean! Our society hinges on the practice of mutual aid and cooperation, whose corollary is generosity. When our chiefs and kings gave acres and acres of land to foreigners they were not prompted by bribes or stupidity but by this selfsame habit of generosity—the lifeblood of our society. Even more precious, I think, is our spirit of kindness. For me to be able to walk into the home of any African between Khartoum and Durban and be certain to be accorded the utmost hospitality is to my mind a pulsating example of what quality of human relationship our society is capable of producing.

Nor is the scope of our kindness limited to our own race. Many are the days when we have preserved the life of one foreigner or another. Times without number we have gone out of our way to hunt for water, eggs, milk, chicken, fish, meat, fruit, and vegetables for a choosy stranger. We have carried literally thousands of foreigners on our heads and shoulders; we have washed their clothes; we have reared their children; we have looked after their homes; we have stood by their sides in peril; we have defended them in times of war; we have given them our land, we have given them our precious minerals, nay, we have given them our all. But the gratitude we often get is ridicule, contempt, ill-treatment, and the belief on their part that God created us to be "hewers of wood and drawers of water." No. God knows our kindness does not stem from a feeling of inferiority. God knows we are not kind because we are fools, but because He ordained that we should be kindness-drunk rather than pride-drunk.

And yet, in spite of all this ingratitude, we are still capable of forgiving and forgetting. We are in a position to do this because in our society forgiveness is the rule rather than the exception. Professor Richard A. Brown has this to say of us:

> The simple spirituality of the Negro and his African brother, their deep-rooted belief in God, their matchless capacity to love and forgive even those who mistreat them, their natural humanity—all these characteristics of these people, tempered and refined in the furnace of trials and tribulations down through the years, are qualities the world stands most in need of in these difficult times. . . .

Another outstanding characteristic of our outlook is our love for music, dance, and rhythm. This three-pronged phenomenon is indeed the spice of our life. Our throats are deep with music, our legs full of dance, while our bodies tremble with rhythm. We sing while we hoe. We sing while we paddle our canoes. Our mourning is in the form of dirges; we sing in bereavement just as on festive occasions. Our fables nearly always include a song. We sing to while away the monotonous hours of travel. . . .

We have war dances, victory dances, remedial dances, marriage dances, dances for women only, mixed dances, dances for the initiated, dances for the young—but all indulged in with ecstatic abandon. We nod our heads, rock our necks, tilt our heads and pause. We shake our shoulders, throw them back and forth, bounce breasts, and halt to intone our thanks to Him who ordained that we be alive. Dance! What a world of emotions that word calls forth in us.

There is rhythm in the winnowing and pounding of grains, there is rhythm in the gait of our womenfolk, . . . there is rhythm in the groan of a sick person, there is complex rhythm in milking a cow or pulling a draw-net to the shore;

there is rhythm that beggars description in the beats of our tom-toms. The difference between us and other peoples is that we consciously cultivate rhythm in almost everything we do.

Finally, we have a strong dislike for imposing our beliefs on other people. British people established themselves over-seas with the self-assuredness of angels. They believed with puritanical fervor that the British way was the God-vouched way of doing things. Their way of living was what mankind was destined to evolve up to; their ideas the Gospel truth; their beliefs the paragons of man's triumph over superstition. No other way—least of all the colonial people's way—could measure up to it, still less be better than it. So they believed there was nothing for them to learn from their colonial subjects, while the colonial [subjects] had to be recast into the British mold of life, thought, and belief.

That was all very well for the purposes of empire building. To rule a people successfully you have got to drill it into their heads that you are in every way superior to them and that, therefore, it is the right thing for them to be under you. But that way of thinking tends to arrest progress. The advancement of man uncompromisingly demands a ceaseless synthesis of ideas, a blending of ways of living, a give and take of beliefs, and above all a willingness to believe that the best is yet to come.

If persisted in, this attitude of finality, superiority, and self-deception can only promote hate and racial discord. When other peoples do not assert themselves, they may still have something to be proud of, something that they believe is unrivalled, but it is just that they have not got the same vulgarity of throwing their weight about and imposing themselves and their beliefs on other people. They are willing to live and let live. Further, they have the satisfaction of knowing that a listener with an open mind has the "open sesame" to the fortune of knowledge and wisdom. There is a great deal that foreigners, in Africa as well as overseas, have to learn from the colonial peoples.

Negritude

❧ INTRODUCTION: The most prominent cultural movement to develop during the nationalist period in Africa was centered around the concept of "Negritude." According to Leopold Sedar Senghor, former President of Senegal and one of the leaders of the movement, "negritude is first of all 'Negro personality,' the fact of being a Negro among other men who are not black. . . . Negritude is the cultural heritage, the values, and above all the *spirit* of Negro-African civilization." Chisiza makes a similar point in the last reading.

Basically, the Negritude movement was—and still is—a literary movement. It developed in French-speaking West Africa in reaction to the French colonial policy of attempting to assimilate Africans into French culture. Faced with the prospect of losing their own culture, West African intellectuals felt compelled to assert and even exaggerate the uniqueness of their African heritage.

In fact, the founders of the movement were already highly assimilated and living far from home, both culturally and geographically. They were students in Paris, and to "keep in touch" they published a literary magazine during 1933-35 which launched the Negritude movement. The leaders were Aimé Cesaire, a West Indian from Martinque, León Dumas, from French Guiana, and Senghor. The word "Negritude" was first used by Césaire in a poem written in 1938.

Some critics claim that Negritude is a racist concept, but Senghor points out:

> The British speak of "Anglo-Saxon civilization" because they are men, and the French speak of "French civilization" or "Greco-Latin civilization." We Negroes speak of Negritude, for we too are men—who, forty thousand years ago, were the first to emerge as *Homo sapiens*, the first men to express themselves in

art, the first to create the earliest agrarian civilization in the valleys of the Nile and of Mesopotamia.

In a sense, Negritude had existed for hundreds of years, wherever black people were forced to live in a foreign culture and attempted to preserve their identity. Many black American writers of the nineteenth and early twentieth centuries expressed Negritudinist ideas, and today the concept of "soul" serves very much the same purpose as Negritude: to preserve and exalt what is special in a cultural tradition. Referring to Cesaire's poetry, Senghor asks: "What is surprising about his using his pen like Louis Armstrong his trumpet? Or more accurately, perhaps, like the devotees of Voodoo their tom-toms? He needs to lose himself in the dance of words, the tom-tom rhythm, to rediscover himself in the Universe."

This last point is important: the concept of Negritude, like nationalism, was a means by which black Africans could claim their place in the universe, a place denied them by outside forces. The following three poems all embody the concept of Negritude in one way or another. They are by black writers, from Haiti[32], Senegal[33], and French Guiana[34], in that order.

African Heart

This tiresome heart, that never fits
my language or my dress,
forced into the straightjacket
of borrowed sentiments and customs,
trifles of Europe. Oh, in my lame despair
I am condemned to tame
my heart that came from Senegal
with foreign words from France.

Africa

Africa my Africa
Africa of proud warriors in the ancestral savannahs
Africa my grandmother sings of
Beside her distant river
I have never seen you
But my gaze is full of your blood
Your black blood spilt over the fields

The Negritude movement encouraged writers and other artists to express an African point of view. Here a young Nigerian painter, Demas Nwoko, shows his conception of a westernized Adam and Eve. Notice that Eve is wearing a fur coat. For a touch of irony, missiles and planes fly in the background. (Marc and Evelyne Bernheim from Rapho Guillumette)

The blood of your sweat
The sweat of your toil
The toil of your slavery
The slavery of your children
Africa, tell me Africa,
Are you the back that bends?
Lies down under the weight of humbleness?
The trembling back striped red
That says yes to the *sjambok* [whip] on the roads of noon?
Solemnly a voice answers me

"Impetuous child, that young and sturdy tree
That tree that grows
There splendidly alone among white and faded flowers
Is Africa, your Africa. It puts forth new shoots
With patience and stubborness puts forth new shoots
Slowly its fruits grow to have
The bitter taste of liberty."

Limbo

. . . Give me back my black dolls. I want to play with them,
Play the ordinary games that come naturally to me,
Stay in the shadow of their rules,
Get back my courage and my boldness,
Feel myself, what I was yesterday,
Without complexity.
Yesterday, when I was torn up by the roots.

Will they ever know the rancor eating at my heart,
My mistrustful eye open too late?
They have stolen the space that was mine
The customs, the days of my life
the singing, the rhythm, the strain,
The path, the water, the hut
The earth, gray, smoky
And wisdom, the words, the palavers,
The ancients.
And the beat, the hands, the beating of the hands
And the stamping of feet on the ground.

Give them back to me, my black dolls,
My black dolls,
Black dolls
Black.

Kenya: The Man and the Elephant

𝔂 INTRODUCTION: Resistance to African demands for independence was strongest in countries that had large communities of white settlers. The settlers' grandparents and great-grandparents had come to Africa—much as immigrants came to America—to find a new place in the sun; they came to stay, and as long as they stayed they planned to rule.

Such a situation existed in Kenya, where in 1934 some two thousand English settlers controlled 6½ million acres of the best land, or approximately 2,530 acres per settler, as compared to only seven acres (of poorer land) per African. The settlers were either given the land outright by the colonial government or bought it for a few cents per acre. They developed this land into profitable coffee and tea plantations and considered the land theirs by right of law and labor; thus they were reluctant to give it back to the Africans.

Most of this land had been taken from the Kikuyu people, farmers living in the fertile highlands of central Kenya. Hence the settler territory became known as the "White Highlands." By 1948 there were 30,000 Europeans living in Kenya, 9,000 of whom were settlers. The Europeans represented less than 1 per cent of the total Kenyan population of 5½ million (today 23 million), but they controlled about 25 per cent of the best land.

While the Europeans were taking their land, the Kikuyu were restricted to reserves too small to support them. Unable to subsist by farming, many Kikuyu were forced to work for white settlers (on land they felt was theirs) or to migrate to the cities, where the colonial government needed labor and domestic help. Indeed, the colonial land grab was a part of a deliberate attempt to make Africans work for the Europeans. (See "The Coming Of The Pink Cheeks" on p. xx)

African laborers fared little better than African farmers. In 1952 their average income was only $74 per year; the Europeans averaged $1,739. Naturally, the Africans, particularly the Kikuyu, objected to

239

This white settler, who controls 5,000 acres of fertile land in Kenya, here negotiates with African squatters who have settled on his land because "we have nowhere else to go." Many Africans who were pushed off their land by whites during the colonial period returned after independence. (Photonews)

such injustices. Colonial commission after colonial commission studied the situation, but nothing was ever done. Finally, in 1952 the desperate and land-starved Kikuyu organized an open rebellion known as Mau Mau. (The phrase "Mau Mau" has no meaning in the Kikuyu language. It was simply the name used derisively by the British to describe the Kikuyu movement for independence that exploded in 1952.)

The following selection, written by the Rev. Ndabaningi Sithole, a prominent Zimbabwean nationalist, contains a fable about the loss of Kikuyu land written by the most famous of all Kikuyu, Jomo Kenyatta, president of Kenya from independence in 1963 to his death in 1978. After spending 15 years in England, where he earned a Ph.D. in anthropology and wrote *Facing Mt. Kenya*, a classic "inside" view of traditional African culture, Kenyatta returned to Africa in 1946 to lead the struggle for Kenyan independence. Kenyatta was jailed from 1952-59 on the charge that he organized the Mau Mau movement, a charge that he consistently denied. Indeed, the man who testified against him was found to have lied during the trial.[35] ❧

We may be excused if we quote at great length, but we feel compelled to do so that we may show what happens when a

legitimate challenge is not met honestly by powers-that-be.
Jomo Kenyatta . . . described relations between the Kikuyu and
the Europeans in Kenya as follows:

An elephant made friendship with a man. Driven by a
heavy thunderstorm, the elephant sought shelter in the man's
hut that was on the edge of the forest. The elephant was allowed
partial admission, but eventually he evicted the man from his
hut and took full possession of the hut, saying: "My dear good
friend, your skin is harder than mine, and there is not enough
room for both of us. You can afford to remain in the rain while I
am protecting my delicate skin from the hailstorm."

A dispute between the elephant and the man ensued. This
attracted the notice of the King of the Jungle. In the interest of
peace and good order the Lion assured the grumbling man that
he would appoint a Commission of Inquiry: "You have done
well by establishing friendship with my people, especially with
the elephant, who is one of my honorable ministers of state. Do
not grumble any more, your hut is not lost to you. Wait until
the sitting of my Imperial Commission, and there you will be
given plenty of opportunity to state your case. I am sure you
will be pleased with the findings of the Commission."

The Commission was duly appointed. It comprised (1) Mr.
Rhinoceros; (2) Mr. Buffalo; (3) Mr. Alligator; (4) The Rt.
Hon. Mr. Fox to act as chairman; and (5) Mr. Leopard to act as
Secretary to the Commission. The man asked that one of his
kind be included on the Commission, but he was assured that
none of his kind was educated enough to understand the
intricacy of jungle law, and that the members of the Commission were God-chosen and would execute their business with
justice.

The elephant gave his evidence: "Gentlemen of the Jungle,
there is no need for me to waste your valuable time in relating a
story which I am sure you all know. I have always regarded it as
my duty to protect the interests of my friends, and this appears
to have caused the misunderstanding between myself and my
friend here. He invited me to save his hut from being blown
away by a hurricane. As the hurricane had gained access owing
the unoccupied space in the hut, I considered it necessary, in my

friend's own interests, to turn the undeveloped space to a more economic use by sitting in it myself; a duty which any of you would undoubtedly have performed with equal readiness in similar circumstances."

Next the man gave interrupted evidence and the Commission delivered its verdict as follows: "In our opinion this dispute has arisen through a regrettable misunderstanding due to the backwardness of your ideas. We consider that Mr. Elephant has fulfilled his sacred duty of protecting your interests. As it is clearly for your good that the space should be put to its economic use, and as you yourself have not yet reached the age of expansion which would enable you to fill it, we consider it necessary to arrange a compromise to suit both parties. Mr. Elephant shall continue his occupation of your hut, but we give you permission to look for a site where you can build another hut more suited to your needs, and we shall see that you are well protected."

The man, fearing exposure to the teeth and claws of the members of the Commission, had no alternative. He built another hut. Mr. Rhinoceros came and occupied it. Another Commission of Inquiry was set up. The man was advised to look for a new site. This went on until all the members of the Commission had been properly housed at the expense of the man. Then the desperate man said to himself, *"Ng' enda thi ndeagaga motegi"* (There is nothing that treads on the earth that cannot be trapped; i.e., You can fool people for a time, but not forever).

So the man built a big hut, and soon the lords of the jungle came and occupied the big hut. The man shut them in and set the hut on fire and all perished. The man returned home, saying: "Peace is costly, but it's worth the expense."

It is interesting to note that the above account was first published in 1938, that is, fourteen years before the Mau Mau Revolt of 1952-55. And in 1952, the Mau Mau did set Kenya on fire in sheer desperation after many British commissions of inquiry had failed to satisfy the Kikuyu. It is also interesting to note that Jomo Kenyatta's *Facing Mount Kenya* is dedicated to:

. . . Moigoi and Wamboi and all the dispossessed youth of
Africa: for perpetuation of communion with ancestral spirits
through the fight for African Freedom, and in the firm faith
that the dead, the living, and the unborn will unite to rebuild
the destroyed shrines.

Whatever the verdict of history may be, for or against
Jomo Kenyatta, the truth remains that he embodied the spirit
of freedom and independence found all over Africa today. He
tried to fight for the Kikuyu to be treated like human beings in
the land of their birth. Everything else failed and a revolution
was the only course open to the Kikuyu. The Mau Mau Revolt
was the only course open to them.

What we are trying to say here is that if the doors of
democracy are deliberately shut against the Africans, some
other hideous alternatives will present themselves to them.

I remember a Briton hotly arguing with an African
politician. "You Africans surprise us. Before the white man
came to Africa, you never clamored for these things. You did
nothing except sleep."

"And while we slept we enjoyed our sleep," replied the
African.

"I suggest very strongly that you resume your sleep, and
stop all this nonsense about African independence," (said the
Briton).

"You can't have it both ways," said the African. "You
must accept the consequences of your own actions. Africa is
astir and it's impossible to resume our sleep."

One African thinker put it this way, "It's not good
expecting an awake African to behave as though he was still
asleep." . . . .

The "Mau Mau" Revolt

✻ INTRODUCTION: A misleading set of beliefs has developed about the "Mau Mau" Revolt. Some critics, mostly Westerners, charge that the violence of the revolt is "typical of African behavior." Nothing could be further from the truth. Most Africans—indeed, the overwhelming majority—did not resort to violence to win independence, despite conditions that history shows would have driven other people to the barricades.

It has also been charged that the "Mau Mau" used violence beyond the demands of the situation, that they practiced a brand of brutality "seldom seen by the world." It is true that the "Mau Mau" used terror against the enemy, attacking at night with knives and fire, but the British used guns and bombs. Why is one side more brutal than the other? Furthermore, during the height of the fighting, between 1953 and 1956, a total of 11,503 Kikuyu (Mau Mau) were killed as compared to only 95 Europeans and 1,920 African "loyalists."

The Mau Mau movement grew out of a militant organization called the Kikuyu Central Association (KCA), which had agitated for independence before World War II but was forced to go underground by the colonial government. After the war, the Kenya African Union (KAU) was formed to serve as a coordinating committee for all nationalist groups. The KCA, working within the KAU, soon came to realize that constitutional reforms, while sanctioned by the British government, were strongly resisted by the white settlers, who looked to South Africa as a model for white control.

To prepare for a possible confrontation with the settlers, the KCA attempted to unify its ranks by requiring its members to take oaths of loyalty. The white settlers saw this oath-taking as a "return to savagery and barbarism," and the colonial government responded by arresting 22 of the most important KCA leaders. By this time (1950), between 75 and 90 per cent of all Kikuyus had allegedly taken the oath.

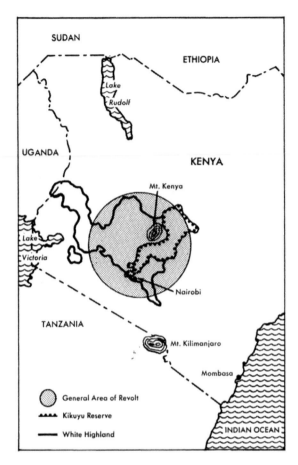

The Kikuyus (or certain local groups) reacted to the ban on oath-taking, and to government attacks on oath-taking ceremonies, by attacking government buildings and police stations. The government announced a "State of Emergency" in early 1952 and declared war on the Kikuyu. During the four years of the Emergency more than 80,000 Kikuyus were detained by the government, not to mention those who were killed or wounded during the actual fighting. The rebellion was eventually suppressed with the help of troops called in from England.

It is clear from the sequence of events that the Mau Mau Revolt was not a pre-planned attack on Europeans but, rather, a reaction to the uncompromising attitude of the white settlers. In a very real sense, the overreaction of the settlers to oath-taking lit the fires of the revolt.

The current world view of Mau Mau is derived mostly from

British reports issued during the revolt as a form of propaganda. The following three-part selection, based on the testimony of Africans who experienced Mau Mau, attempts to provide some counterbalance for that lopsided view. The selection is by no means intended as an apology for Mau Mau; killing is inhuman no matter who practices it. Rather, it is intended to bring some light to a dark episode in Africa's struggle for independence.

The first of the three selections, "The Awakening," tells how Kenyatta stirred nationalist feeling; "The Oath" illustrates the values that unified the Kikuyu people; "The Raids" describes some of the Mau Mau attacks.[36] ❧

THE AWAKENING

It was 26 July 1952 and I sat in the Nyeri Showgrounds packed in with a crowd of over 30,000 people. The Kenya African Union (KAU) was holding a rally and it was presided over by Jomo Kenyatta. He talked first of LAND. In the Kikuyu country, nearly half of the people are landless and have an earnest desire to acquire land so that they can have something to live on.

Kenyatta pointed out that there was a lot of land lying idly in the country and only the wild game enjoy that, while Africans are starving. . . . The White Highlands, he went on, together with the forest reserves which were under the government control, were taken from the Africans unjustly. . . .

The other point that Jomo Kenyatta stressed during the meeting was African FREEDOM. He raised the KAU flag to symbolize African government. He said Kenya must be freed from colonial exploitation. Africa must be given freedom of speech, freedom of movement, freedom of worship and freedom of press. Explaining this to the people, he said that with the exception of freedom of worship, . . . freedoms are severely limited with respect to the Africans. . . . Many Africans have been prosecuted for trespassing on European land or for entering a town outside their own district. I personally faced a resident magistrate, the D.C. (District Commissioner) at Nnanyuki, in December 1949 charged with trespass on a European

The late Jomo Kenyatta, former President of Kenya, led the nationalist movement in his country. He was accused of organizing the Mau Mau, but there is no reliable evidence to support this claim. The beaded cap he wears indicates that Kenyatta is Kikuyu. (Marc and Evelyne Bernheim from Rapho Guillumette)

farm. Without a fine, he sentenced me to three month's imprisonment. He refused to [allow me to pay] money for the sentence.

I was struck by the flag's red color in the middle of black and green, which signified blood. An hour passed without any description of the KAU flag. Most of the time I was pondering how and when we shall officially hoist that National flag to signify the Kenya African freedom. I recalled Kenyatta's words in 1947 at a KAU rally on the same ground. "The freedom tree can only grow when you pour blood on it, but not water. I shall firmly hold the lion's jaws so that it will not bite you. Will you bear its claws?" [He was answered with great applause.]

When Kenyatta returned [to] the platform for the third time, after a few other speakers, he explained the flag. He said, "Black is to show that this is for black people. Red is to show that the blood of an African is the same color as as the blood of a European. And green is to show that when we were given this country by God it was green, fertile and good but now you see the green is below the red and is suppressed." (Tremendous applause!) I tried to figure out his real meaning. What was meant by green being "suppressed" and below the red? Special Branch agents [of the government] were at the meeting recording all the speeches so Kenyatta couldn't speak his mind directly. What he said must mean that our fertile lands (green) could only be regained by the blood (red) of the African (black). That was it! The black was separated from the green by red; the African could only get his land through blood. . . .

THE OATH

I swear before God and before all the people present here that

(1) I shall never reveal this secret of the KCA oath—which is of Kikuyu and Mumbi and which demands land and freedom —to any person who is not a member of our society. If I ever reveal it, may this oath kill me! (Repeated after each vow while biting the chest meat of a billy goat held together with the heart and lungs.)

(2) I shall always help any member of our society who is in difficulty or need of help.

(3) If I am ever called, during the day or night, to do any work for this society, I shall obey.

(4) I shall on no account ever disobey the leaders of this society.

(5) If I am ever given firearms or ammunition to hide, I shall do so.

(6) I shall always give money or goods to this society whenever called upon to do so.

(7) I shall never sell land to a European or an Asian.

A British officer, supported by African police, searches a Mau Mau suspect. More than 11,000 Kikuyu were killed between 1952 and 1956. (Photoworld, Inc.)

(8) I shall not permit intermarriage between Africans and the white community.

(9) I will never go with a prostitute.

(10) I shall never cause a girl to become pregnant and leave her unmarried.

(11) I will never marry and then seek a divorce.

(12) I shall never allow any daughter to remain uncircumcised.

(13) I shall never [use] European-manufactured beer or cigarettes.

(14) I shall never spy on or otherwise sell my people to Government.

(15) I shall never help the missionaries in their Christian faith to ruin our traditional and cultural customs.

(16)   I will never accept the Beecher Report [an education plan considered detrimental to African children].

(17) I shall never steal any property belonging to a member of our society.

(18) I shall obey any strike call, whenever notified.

(19) I will never retreat or abandon any of our mentioned demands but will daily increase more and stronger demands until we acheive our goals.

(20) I shall pay 62/50s. and a ram as assessed by this society as soon as I am able.

(21) I shall always follow the leadership of Jomo Kenyatta and Mbiyu Koinange.

THE RAIDS

On the night of 26 March 1953 two well-organized Mau Mau raids took place at Naivasha and Lari. The Naivasha raid was on a police post which was taken by surprise. After a short time of exchanging fire, the police guards ran away. Our warriors entered the camp, released all the prisoners, broke into the armory, and made off with all the arms and ammunition.

According to Government's report, our warriors gained 47 precision weapons, including 18 Bren and Sten guns, and 3,780 rounds of ammunition. Our warriors claimed to have gained over 100 precision weapons from the Naivasha raid. . . .

This raid increased the strength and fame of Mau Mau. I thought they must have had good plans. The other raid was on Chief Luka of Lari and his supporters. The plan was successful. He and his wives were killed and their houses set on fire. I learned from friends who witnessed that in the morning the Government killed ten times as many persons as the ones who had been killed and set houses on fire. It was then claimed that the whole action had been committed by Mau Mau, in which more than 100 men, women, and children had been killed. As I looked at it, there were two motives behind the Government action.

The first, a revenge which, by being uncontrolled, went beyond their intentions. The second, to disdain Mau Mau for the mercilessly unjust killing of women and children, thereby

Mutinous troops of the Kenya Rifles, the African branch of the British Army in Kenya, are shown being marched back to their barracks at gun point. Several mutinies took place during the State of Emergency, and a total of 80,000 Africans were "detained." (London Daily Express)

causing the sympathizers to think that the Mau Mau have lost sight of their enemies and have started killing the innocent ones and that probably the following day would be their turn. This only meant to cover [conceal] the Mau Mau aims by a horrible action to the eyes of the people.

I personally sympathized with the innocent children [who died] no matter which side killed them. But the blame cast on Mau Mau to the world by Government for the action was unfair and [false propaganda]. It only made me think that the British believe that killing by a gun or bomb is right, while killing with a *panga* [machete] is evil. To me, it made no difference whatsoever.

But who has killed more innocent women and children, British or Mau Mau? I wondered whether the bombs dropped on towns and cities by the British during the First and Second World Wars—and in their many other wars—spared the lives of the inncoent women and children for which they were blaming us. And who dropped the atomic bomb on Hiroshima? How many died? Compare them with the "Lari massacre."

Radio, press, and films were used to inform the world of the barbarous, uncivilized Lari massacre. Yes, uncivilized— but the British haven't stopped it [*i.e.*, uncivilized killing of innocent people]. Neither have the civilized French, who have been killing innocent women and children in Algeria for over seven years, stopped it. This left me with the thought that the British were either blind to their own errors while they were bright in exposing their opponents' mistakes, or they were doing it deliberately for their selfish injustices.

The Martyr

🌿 INTRODUCTION: The flames of Mau Mau raged from 1952 to 1956, when the "State of Emergency" was finally brought to a close. Kenyans then returned to more peaceful forms of political activity and finally, on December 12, 1963, won their independence from England.

In the excitement of mass political movements, especially sensational ones like Mau Mau, individuals get lost. But, after all, it is *for* individuals that movements are formed, and it is individuals who are most affected by violence. The next reading, a short story, focuses on the lives of a few individuals, both African and European, who become "victimized" by the struggle for independence in Kenya. The author, Ngugi wa Thiong'o, is one of Kenya's best-known writers.[37] 🌿

When Mr. and Mrs. Garstone were murdered in their home by unknown gangsters, there was a lot of talk about it. It was all on the front page of the daily papers and figured importantly in the Radio Newsreel. Perhaps this was so because they were the first European settlers to be killed in the increased wave of violence that had spread all over the country. The violence was said to have political motives. And wherever you went, in the marketplaces, in the Indian bazaars, in a remote African *duka* [shop], you were bound to hear something about the murder. There were a variety of accounts and interpretations.

Nowhere was the matter more thoroughly discussed than in a remote, lonely house built on a hill, which belonged, quite appropriately, to Mrs. Hill, whose husband, an old veteran

settler of the pioneering period, had died the previous year
after an attack of malaria, while on a visit to Uganda. Her only
son and daughter were now getting their education at "home"
—home being another name for England. Being one of the
earliest settlers and owning a lot of land with big tea
plantations sprawling right across the country, she was much
respected by the others if not liked by all.

For some did not like what they considered her too-
"liberal" attitude to the "natives." When Mrs. Smiles and Mrs.
Hardy came into her house two days later to discuss the
murder, they wore a look of sad triumph—sad because
Europeans (not just Mr. and Mrs. Garstone) had been killed,
and of triumph, because the essential depravity and ingratitude of the natives had been demonstrated beyond all doubt.
No longer could Mrs. Hill maintain that natives could be
civilized if only they were handled in the right manner.

* * *

"That's all they need. *Treat them kindly.* They will take
kindly to you. Look at my 'boys.' They all love me. They
would do anything I ask them to!"

That was her philosophy, and it was shared by quite a
number of liberal, progressive types. Mrs. Hill had done some
liberal things to her "boys." Not only had she built some brick
quarters (*brick*, mind you) but had also put up a school for the
children. It did not matter if the school had not enough
teachers or if the children learned only a half a day and worked
in the plantations for the other half; it was more than most
other settlers had the courage to do!

"It is horrible. Oh, a horrible act," declared Mrs. Smiles
rather vehemently. Mrs. Hardy agreed. Mrs. Hill remained
neutral.

"How could they do it? We've brought 'em civilization.
We stopped slavery and tribal wars. Were they not all leading
savage, miserable lives?" Mrs. Smiles spoke with all her powers

of oratory. Then she concluded with a sad shake of the head. "But I've always said they'll never be civilized, simply can't take it."

"We should show tolerance," suggested Mrs. Hill. Her tone spoke more of the missionary than Mrs. Smiles' looks.

"Tolerant! Tolerant! How long shall we continue being tolerant? Who could have been more tolerant than the Garstones? Who more kind? And to think of all the squatters they maintained!"

"Well, it isn't the squatters who—"

"Who did? Who did?"

"They should all be hanged!" suggested Mrs. Hardy. There was conviction in her voice.

"And to think they were actually called from bed by their houseboy!"

"Indeed?"

"Yes. It was their houseboy who knocked at their door and urgently asked them to open. Said some people were after him—"

"Perhaps there—"

"No! It was all planned. All a trick. As soon as the door was opened, the gang rushed in. It's all in the paper."

Mrs. Hill looked away rather guiltily. She had not read her paper.

It was time for tea. She excused herself and went near the door and called out in a kind, shrill voice,

"Njoroge! Njoroge!"

Njoroge was her houseboy. He was a tall, broad-shouldered person nearing middle age. He had been in the Hills' service for more than ten years. He wore green trousers with a red clothband round the waist and a red fez on the head. He now appeared at the door and raised his eyebrows in inquiry—an action which with him accompanied the words "Yes, Memsahib?" [Yes, Madam] or "Ndio, Bwana." [Yes, Master].

"Leta chai" [Bring tea].

"Ndio, Memsahib!" and he vanished back after casting a quick glance round all the memsahibs there assembled. The

conversation which had been interrupted by Njoroge's appearance was now resumed.

"They look so innocent," said Mrs. Hardy.

"Yes. Quite the innocent flower but the serpent under it."
Mrs. Smiles was acquainted with Shakespeare.

"Been with me for ten years or so. Very faithful. Likes me
very much." Mrs. Hill was defending her boy.

"All the same I don't like him. I don't like his face."

"The same with me."

* * *

Supper was over. That ended Njoroge's day. He stepped
out of the light into the countless shadows and then vanished
into the darkness. He was following the footpath from Mrs.
Hill's house to the workers' quarters down the hill. He tried to
whistle to dispel the silence and loneliness that hung around
him. He could not. Instead he heard the owl cry.

He stopped, stood stock-still. Below, he could perceive
nothing. But behind him, the immense silhouette of Memsahib's house—large, imposing—could be seen. He looked back
intently, angrily. In his anger, he suddenly thought he was
growing old.

"You. You. I've lived with you so long. And you've
reduced me to this! In my own land! What have I got from you
in return?" Njoroge wanted to shout to the house all this and
many other things that had long accumulated in his heart. The
house would not respond. He felt foolish and moved on.

Again the owl cried. Twice!

"A warning to her," Njoroge thought. And again his
whole soul rose in anger—anger against all those with a white
skin, all those foreign elements that had displaced the true sons
of the land from their God-given place. Had God not promised
Gekoyo that he would give all the land to the father of the tribe
—he and his posterity? Now all the land had been taken
away.

He remembered his father as he always did when these

moments of anger and bitterness possessed him. He had died in the struggle—the struggle to rebuild the destroyed shrines. That was at the famous Nairobi Massacre when police fired on a people peacefully demonstrating for their right. His father was among the people who died. Since then Njoroge had had to struggle for a living—seeking employment here and there on European farms. He had met many types—some harsh, some kind, but all dominating, giving him just what salary they thought fit for him. Then he had come to be employed by the Hills. It was a strange coincidence that he had come here. A big portion of the land now occupied by Mrs. Hill was the land his father had always shown him as belonging to the family. They had found the land occupied when his father and some of the others had temporarily retired to Muranga owing to famine. They have come back and *Ng'o!* [presto!] the land was gone.

"Do you see that fig tree? Remember that land is yours. Be patient. Watch these Europeans. They will go and then you can claim the land."

He was then small. After his father's death, Njoroge had forgotten all about this injunction. But when he coincidentally came here and saw the tree, he had remembered. He knew it all—all by heart. He knew where every boundary went through.

Njoroge had never liked Mrs. Hill. He had always resented her complacency in thinking she had done so much for the workers. He had worked with cruel types, like Mrs. Smiles and Mrs. Hardy. But he always knew where he stood with such. But Mrs. Hill! Her liberalism was almost smothering. Njoroge hated all settlers. He hated above all what he thought was their hypocrisy and self-satisfaction. He knew that Mrs. Hill was no exception. She was like all the others, only she loved paternalism. It convinced her she was better than the others. But she was worse. You did not know exactly where you stood with her.

All of a sudden, Njoroge shouted, "I hate them! I hate them!" Then a grim satisfaction came over him. Tonight,

White settlers controlled most of the best land of Kenya while Africans provided the labor. This "master-slave" relationship, illustrated here and in "The Martyr," led to sharp conflicts and finally to the Mau Mau Revolt. (International Film Foundation)

anyway, Mrs. Hill would die—pay for her own smug liberalism or paternalism and pay for all the sins of her settlers' race. It would be one settler less.

He came to his own room. All the other rooms belonging to the other workers had stopped smoking. The lights had even gone out in many of them. Perhaps, some were already asleep or gone to the Native Reserve to drink beer. He lit the lantern and sat on the bed. It was a very small room. Sitting on the bed one could almost touch all the corners of the room if one stretched the arms afar. Yet it was here, *here,* that he with two wives and a number of children had to live, had in fact lived for more than five years. So crammed! Yet Mrs. Hill thought that she had done enough by just having the houses built with brick.

"*Mzuri sana,* eh?" (very good, eh?) she was very fond of

asking. And whenever she had visitors she brought them to the edge of the hill and pointed at the houses.

Again Njoroge smiled grimly to think now Mrs. Hill would pay for all this self-congratulatory piety. He also knew that he had an axe to grind. He had to avenge the death of his father and strike a blow for the occupied family land. . . .

* * *

And he realized, all too suddenly, that he could not do it. He could not tell how, but Mrs. Hill, had suddenly crystallized into a woman, a wife, somebody like Njen or Wambuu, and above all, a mother. He could not kill a woman. He could not kill a mother. He hated himself for this change. He felt agitated.

He tried hard to put himself in the other condition, his former self and see her as just a settler. As a settler, it was all easy. For Njoroge hated settlers and all Europeans. If only he could see her like this (as one among many white men or settlers) then he could do it. Without scruples.

But he could not bring back the other self. Not now, anyway. You see, he had never thought of her in these terms. Never! never! Until today. And yet he knew she was the same, and would be the same tomorrow—a patronizing, complacent woman. It was then that he knew that he was a divided man and perhaps would ever remain like that. For now it even seemed an impossible thing to snap just like that ten years of relationship, even though to him they had been years of pain and shame. He prayed and wished there had never been injustices. Then there would never have been this rift—the rift between white and black. Then he would never have been put in this painful situation.

What was he to do now? Would he betray the "boys"? . . .

He went out.

Darkness still covered him and he could see nothing clearly. The stars above seemed to be anxiously awaiting

Njoroge's decision. Then, as if their cold stare was compelling him, he began to walk, walk back to Mrs. Hill's house. He had decided to save her. Then probably he would go to the forest. There, he would forever fight with freer conscience. That seemed excellent. It would also serve as a propitiation for his betrayal of the other "boys."

There was no time to lose. It was already late and the "boys" might come any time. So he ran with one purpose—to save the woman. At the road he heard footsteps. He stepped into the bush and lay still. He was certain that those were the "boys." He waited breathlessly for the footsteps to die. Again he hated himself for this betrayal. But how could he fail to hearken to this voice—the true Voice that speaks to all men and women of all races and all times. He ran on when the footsteps had died. It was necessary to run for, if the "boys" discovered his betrayal, he would surely meet death. But then he did not mind this. He only wanted to finish this other task first.

At last, sweating and panting, he reached Mrs. Hill's house and knocked at the door, crying, "Memsahib! Memsahib!"

Mrs. Hill had not yet gone to bed. She had sat up, a multitude of thoughts crossing her mind. Ever since that afternoon's conversation with the other women, she had felt more and more uneasy. When Njoroge went and she was left alone she had gone to her safe and taken out her pistol, with which she was now toying. It was better to be prepared. It was unfortunate that her husband had died. He might have kept her company.

She sighed over and over again as she remembered her pioneering days. She and her husband and others had tamed the wilderness of this country and had developed a whole mass of unoccupied land. People like Njoroge now lived contented without a single worry about tribal wars. They had a lot to thank the European for.

Yet she did not like those politicians who came to corrupt the otherwise obedient and hard-working men, especially when treated kindly. She did not like this murder of the

Garstones. No! She did not like it. And when she remembered the fact that she was really alone, she thought it might be better for her to move down to Nairobi or Kinangop and stay with friends a while.

But what would she do with her boys? Leave them there? She wondered. She thought of Njoroge. A queer boy. Had he many wives? Had he a large family? It was surprising even to her to find that she had lived with him so long, yet had never thought of him as a man with a family. She had always seen him as a servant. Even now it seemed ridiculous to think of her houseboy as a father with a family. She sighed. This was an omission, something to be righted in the future.

And then she heard a knock on the front door and a voice calling out "Memsahib! Memsahib!"

It was Njoroge's voice. Her houseboy. Sweat appeared all over her face. She could not even hear what the boy was saying, for all the circumstances of the Garstones' death came to her. This was her end. The end of the road. So Njoroge had led them here! She trembled and felt weak.

But all of a sudden, strength came back to her. She knew she was alone. She knew they would break in. No! She would die bravely. Holding her pistol more firmly in her hand, she opened the door and quickly fired. Then a nausea came to her. She had killed a man for the first time. She felt weak and fell down crying. "Come and kill me!" She did not know that she had in fact killed her savior. Njoroge was dead.

On the following day, it was all in the papers. That a single woman could fight a gang fifty strong was bravery unknown. And to think she had killed one too!

Mrs. Smiles and Mrs. Hardy were especially profuse in their congratulations.

"We told you they're all bad."

"They are all bad," agreed Mrs. Hardy. Mrs. Hill kept quiet. The whole circumstances of Njoroge's death still worried her. The more she thought about it, the more of a puzzle it was to her. She gazed still into space. Then she let out a slow enigmatic sigh.

"Don't know?"

"Yes. That's it. Inscrutable." Mrs. Smiles was triumphant.
"All of them should be whipped," agreed Mrs. Hardy.

Perhaps none would ever know that Njoroge was a martyr.
Nor would anyone ever know that Mrs. Hill felt remorse.

Reflections of a Leader

❧ INTRODUCTION: Unlike Kenya, most African countries used nonviolent methods for winning independence. A leading exponent of the nonviolent approach was Kenneth Kaunda, now President of Zambia, who led his country to independence in 1964. In the following selection, Kaunda looks back on his career, recalling incidents and influences that shaped his life and therefore the life of his country. When this was written, in 1963, Kaunda was Minister of Local Government and Social Welfare in Northern Rhodesia, as Zambia was called during the colonial period.[38] ❧

At the beginning of 1960 I was still a prisoner of Her Majesty's Government; the political party I led then had been outlawed, and I was the subject of many abusive statements from high places. Today [1963], I find myself one of Her Majesty's Ministers; since 1960 I have met and talked with Mr. Harold Macmillan, Mr. Butler, President Kennedy and various other world figures. That is a long journey in a short time and it does not give a man much time to think and brood on political subjects . . . .

Let me start by setting out my early history, for it is in those first years that I find the seeds of my present political philosophy and my understanding of the needs of my own country. I look back with deep gratitude to my early years, which I spent at Lubwa, a mission station of the Church of Scotland in the Northern Province of Northern Rhodesia [Zambia]. My father, David Kaunda, was an evangelist who came to Northern Rhodesia from Livingstonia in Nyasaland. My mother, who is still living in the Chinsale District, is a

Kenneth Kaunda, President of Zambia, waves to welcoming crowds at Lusaka Airport. (United Press International)

woman of deep spiritual understanding, and what I know of the Christian faith I learned from her. I think I can say in all honesty that the one thing which influenced me more than any other in the first years of my life was the deep Christian faith of my parents, and the fact that I was living in a community on the Mission Station which was based on love, friendship and kindness. I think it is important to emphasize this point because it was a spiritual and psychological shock to me when I left my home and the Mission Station and found myself facing the hard realities of society in Northern Rhodesia. . . .

As a young man the two books which had the greatest influence on me were *The Life of Abraham Lincoln* and Arthur Mee's *Talks to Boys*. I realized that if a person is to get anywhere in life he will have to struggle; it was the courage and the bravery of Abraham Lincoln and the people who are described in Arthur Mee's books which impressed me most. I hated suffering, not for myself but for others. Always when I saw another suffer, whether it was a child or a man, whether it was an African or a European, I found myself wanting to protest. I remember as a schoolboy that I used to go to the house of a certain master at the school who came to teach us from South Africa. As I swept his floor and dusted his books I would hear him talking about the sufferings of his own people in South Africa and how the only solution would be a political solution.

When I went to Mufulira as a teacher and boarding master at the school there, I was soon found that my best subject in teaching was civics. I became deeply interested in the subject myself, and of course I found that my students were more attentive in that class than in any other. At that time, even as now, I was a great believer in self-help. My civics lessons did not finish in the classroom. I would persuade young boys who had no school fees to make their own little gardens to grow cabbages to sell in the market and find money.

All the time I was becoming more and more oppressed by the sufferings which I saw round about me. Even though on the Copper Mines good wages were paid in comparison with wages in the rural areas, still there was great poverty every-where, and hardly a day passed but I saw one of my fellow Africans suffering some indignity at the hands of the European settler community.

There was one shop in the town of Mufulira which was notorious for its color bar. It was a Chemist [drugstore]. While the European women stood at the counter buying their expensive perfumes and medicines, a long line of African servants queued at the window and often not only were kept waiting but when their turn came to be served were rudely treated by the shop assistants. I determined to make a public protest against this kind of thing, so I deliberately went one day into the main shop and did not queue up with the other Africans at the pigeonhole in the wall. I made no secret of what I was about to do, and many of the schoolboys in my class followed me to the chemist shop and waited outside to see what would happen when I went in.

I dressed myself as best I could and simply went into the

shop and asked the Manager politely for some medicine. As soon as he saw me standing in the place where only European customers were allowed to stand he shouted at me, *"Hamba lapa side."* He was using a language which we know as "kitchen kfaffir;" it is not a real language, it is a bastard language which is only used by an employer when speaking to his servants. I speak my own wonderful language Chibamba, and English, but I do not either speak or attempt to understand "kitchen kaffir," so I stood at the counter and politely requested in English that I should be served. The chemist became exasperated and said to me in English, "If you stand there till Christmas I will never serve you." Since it was the month of April I should have had to remain there a very long time so I said to him, "I intend to report this matter to the District Commissioner."

I went to the District Commissioner's office. Fortunately the District Commissioner was out, for he was one of the old school; however, I saw a young District Officer who was a friend of mine. He was very concerned to hear my story and told me that if ever I wanted anything more from the Chemist all I had to do was to come to him personally and he would buy my medicine for me. I protested that that was not good enough; why should I have to buy my medicine through a European friend?

I asked him to accompany me back to the chemist shop and to make a protest to the Manager. This he did, and I well remember him saying to the Manager, "Here is Mr. Kaunda who is a responsible member of the Urban Advisory Council, and a member of the African Provincial Council. One day he may be a member of the Legislative Council, and you treat him like a common servant." The Manager of the chemist shop apologized and said, "If only he had introduced himself and explained who he was then of course I should have given him proper service."

I had to explain once again that he had missed my point. Why should I have to introduce myself every time I went into a shop . . . any more than I should have to buy my medicine by

Keeping posted on their rapid advance toward democracy and independence, these Nigerian voters cluster around a large board showing results of a parliamentary election. (United Press International)

going to a European friend? I wanted to prove that any man of any color whatever his position should have the right to go into any shop and buy what he wanted. After all, the money which I paid across the counter was exactly the same money as is paid by the European customer.

There I let the matter rest, but some weeks later I went again into that chemist shop to see what reception I would get. The Manager had changed and for the second time I was greeted with the words, "Boy, *hamba lapa side*." Again I stood my ground, but this time there were three large European miners in the shop who did not wait for me to go to the District Commissioner; they simply took hold of me and threw me out into the street, where my friends were waiting and a fight began. However, before long the three Europeans ran off to their car and escaped before the police could be called.

It was during these days that I realized that if Africans were to have their human rights in their own country they could not achieve them by asking anybody else to fight their . . . battles
. . . .

* * *

As a political organizer in Central Africa . . . I found Africans everywhere being treated in their own country as second-class citizens. The reason for this was that the settler, by virtue of his economic strength, had gained complete political control. Democracy became a mockery through the vast gulf between African and white wages. The difference was usually about £15 paid to a white for every £1 given to a black worker. The highly qualitative franchise in Central Africa virtually rendered every European a voter on the basis of one man, one vote, while it effectively excluded Africans. The ownership of property helped to qualify the European for the vote, but all the land that was owned by Africans never counted for [their] property. By custom the land was owned communally and therefore could not be claimed by an individual African . . . even though he built his house on it and grew his food on it.

The whole . . . arrangement was un-Christian and unethical. It contained the seeds of hatred, suspicion, and fear. It was useless to preach racial harmony where such a situation existed. Africans like myself, involved in politics, battled against a huge wall of frustration for "one man, one vote."
. . .

* * *

Independence has given all of Africa a new sense of identity,
as illustrated by this meeting of the Organization of African
Unity. (Rapho Guillumette)

I believe in fundamental human rights. I hold with the American Founding Fathers "that all men are created equal, that they are endowed by their Creator with certain inalienable rights, that among these are life, liberty and the pursuit of happiness." When we are in power this will be our guiding philosophy, and therefore the members of no race need fear victimization or oppression. And I should add that the United National Independence Party does not exclude anyone of any race from its membership, provided he or she accepts our aims and policies and would be a suitable member in other ways.

We in the United National Independence Party are not concerned solely with the rights of Africans; we are struggling for human rights—the inalienable rights of all men. We have engaged in a struggle against any form of imperialism and colonialism not because it has as its agents white men but because it has many more wrong sides than good ones. Temptations in its trends include the one worst form of constitutional arrangement—namely, the concentration of powers in the hands of a small minority over the majority. It is an arrangement that will corrupt the best of men regardless of their color, creed or religion. It is a system that tempts the privileged few to discriminate against the majority who are the have-nots.

The more I ponder . . . this issue, the more I [am] convinced that I am right in refusing to believe that white men do what they do against Africans because they are wicked. They are in power and power corrupts. We have no justification for fighting against our present form of oppression if when in power we turn on our oppressors and subject them to the same indignities we suffer at their hands. Our moral and Christian right to fight against the Government of our country rests on a determination to replace it with a system that is grounded in Christian belief that all men are born equal in the sight of God.

* * *

I believe that Africa has a unique place in determining the future of world affairs as long as it keeps free of power blocs. I have visited the United States of America, Britain, and many European countries, and although I have never been to Russia, it is my impression that in both the East and West there are people who have become enslaved by their possessions. It is only in Africa that I find real sanity, for I believe that the African people, whether they live in East Africa, Central Africa, or South Africa, have still retained a simplicity and a closeness to God and the earth which enables them to treat each other as human beings. I find this a matter which is very difficult to explain, but I know that when I talk to my friend

Julius Nyerere [former President of Tanzania] we have something in common which I do not have when I talk with people from the Western world. I would almost go so far to say that in its search for wealth and power, the West has lost its soul. I believe that Africans and Africa have a great mission, that is, to remain neutral in the struggle which is going on between East and West and to show a better way, which is being discovered by those who weave together their Christian faith and their African humanity.

Africa is now striving for unity . . . . Of course, there will be setbacks and mistakes in the cooperation and advancement of Africa's peoples. However, I am convinced that if the world is spared a nuclear catastrophe, Africa will contribute much to the sum of world happiness and enlightenment in the second half of the twentieth century.

Independence Ledger

Date of Independence	Country (Former Name)	Capital	Colonizer
May 31, 1910*	South Africa*	Pretoria	Britain
December 24, 1951	Republic of Libya (Libya)	Tripoli	Italy
January 1, 1956	Republic of the Sudan (Anglo-Egyptian Sudan)	Khartoum	Britain/ Egypt
March 2, 1956/1969	Kingdom of Morocco (Morocco)	Rabat	France/ Spain
March 6, 1957	Republic of Ghana (Gold Coast and Togoland)	Accra	Britain
March 20, 1956	Republic of Tunisia (Tunisia)	Tunis	France
October 2, 1958	Republic of Guinea (French Guinea)	Conakry	France
January 1, 1960	Federal Republic of Cameroon (French Cameroons and South British Cameroons)	Yaounde	France/ Britain
April 27, 1960	Republic of Togo (French Togoland)	Lomé	Germany/ France
June 20, 1960	Republic of Mali (Soudan, Part of Federation of Mali)	Bamako	France
June 27, 1960	Malagasy Republic (Madagascar)	Antananarivo	France

*South Africa gained its independence from Great Britain in 1910 and became the Union of South Africa; it broke away from the British Commonwealth in 1961 and became the Republic of South Africa. Throughout its modern political history, South Africa has been controlled by a white minority government, representing today only 13 percent of the total population.

June 30, 1960	Zaire (Congo)	Kinshasa	Belgium
July 1, 1960	Somali Republic (Somalia and British Somaliland)	Mogadishu	Britain/ Italy
August 1, 1960	Benin (Republic of Dahomey)	Porto Novo	France
August 3, 1960	Republic of Niger (Niger)	Niamey	France
August 5, 1960	Burkina Faso (Upper Volta)	Ouagadougou	France
August 7, 1960	Republic of Ivory Coast Cote d'Ivoire (Ivory Coast)	Abidjan	France
August 11, 1960	Republic of Chad (Chad)	Ndjamena	France
August 13, 1960	Central African Republic (Oubangi-Chari)	Bangui	France
August 15, 1960	Republic of Congo (Brazzaville, Middle Congo)	Brazzaville	France
August 17, 1960	Gabon Republic (Gabon)	Libreville	France
August 20, 1960	Republic of Senegal (Senegal, Part of Federation of Mali)	Dakar	France
October 1, 1960	Federal Republic of Nigeria (Nigeria)	Lagos	Britain
November 28, 1960	Islamic Republic of Mauritania (Mauritania)	Nouakchott	France
April 27, 1961	Sierra Leone	Freetown	Britain
December 9, 1961	United Republic of Tanzania (Tanganyika and Zanzibar)	Dar Es Salaam	Britain
July 1, 1962	Kingdom of Burundi (Ruanda-*Urundi*)	Bujumbura	Germany/ Belgium
July 1, 1962	Republic of Ruanda (*Rwanda*-Urundi)	Kigali	Germany/ Belgium
July 3, 1962	Democratic and Popular Republic of Algeria (Algeria)	Algiers	France
October 9, 1962	Uganda	Kampala	Britain

December 12, 1963	Republic of Kenya (Kenya)	Nairobi	Britain
July 6, 1964	Malawi (Nyasaland)	Liliongwe	Britain
October 24, 1964	Republic of Zambia (Northern Rhodesia)	Lusaka	Britain
February 18, 1965	The Gambia (Gambia)	Banjul (Bathurst)	Britain
September 30, 1966	Botswana (Bechuanaland)	Gabarone	Britain
October 4, 1966	Lesotho (Basutoland)	Maseru	Britain
March 12, 1968	Mauritius	Port Louis	Britain
September 6, 1968	Swaziland	Mbabane	Britain
October 12, 1968	Equatorial Guinea	Malabo	Spain
September 10, 1974	Guinea-Bissau (Portuguese Guinea)	Bissau	Portugal
February 28, 1975	Western Sahara (Spanish Sahara)	Elaaium	Spain
June 25, 1975	Mozambique	Maputo	Portugal
July 5, 1975	Cape Verde Islands	Praia	Portugal
July 6, 1975	Comoro Islands	Moroni	France
July 12, 1975	Sao Tome & Principe	Sao Tome	Portugal
November 11, 1975	Angola	Luanda	Portugal
June 26, 1976	Seychelles	Victoria	Britain
June 27, 1977	Djibouti (French Somaliland)	Djibouti	France
April 18, 1980	Zimbabwe (Southern Rhodesia)	Harare	Britain
March 21, 1990	Namibia (South West Africa)	Windhoek	Germany/ South Africa

(NOTE: Three independent countries are not included in the Ledger: Ethiopia, Liberia, and the United Arab Republic. Ethiopia has never been colonized; Libera was established as an American protectorate for repatriated Afro-American slaves and became independent in 1847; Egypt [The United Arab Republic] regained its independence from England in 1922.)

SOURCES

1. Luis Bernardo Honwana, "The Hands of the Blacks." Trans. by Dorothy Guedes. *New York Times Magazine*, April 30, 1967, pp. 26-27 Copyright © 1967 by The New York Times Company. Reprinted by permission of The New York Times Company and the Author.
2. Leon E. Clark, *Through African Eyes*, Vol. 3, New York: Praeger Publisher, 1970, pp. 8-18.
3. Kwame Nkrumah, *I Speak Freedom* New York: Praeger, 1961, pp. 67-68.
4. Ibn Fadl Allah al Omari, *Masalik al Absar Fi Mamalik al Amsar.* Trans. by Basil Davidson, from the French version of Gaudefroy-Demombynes (Paris, 1927). Reprinted from *The African Past* by Basil Davidson. Boston: Little, Brown & Co., 1964, pp. 75-79. Copyright © 1964 by Basil Davidson. Reprinted by permission of Atlantic-Little, Brown & Co. and the Longman Group Ltd.

   Ibn Battuta, *Travels in Asia and Africa: 1325-1354.* Trans. by Sir Hamilton Gibb. London: Routledge & Kegan Paul Ltd., 1929, pp. 326-329. Reprinted by permission of the publisher.

   Ibn Battuta, *Travels in Asia and Africa: 1325-1354.* Trans. by Basil Davidson, from the French version of Defremery and Sanguinetti (Paris, 1854). Reprinted from *The African Past*, by Basil Davidson. Boston: Little, Brown & Co., 1964, pp. permission of Atlantic-Little, Brown & Co. and the Longman Group Ltd.
5. D.T. Niane, *Sundiata: An Epic of Old Mali.* Translated by G.D. Pickett. London: Longman, Green & Co., Ltd., 1965, pp. 1-3, 83-84. (Originally published by Presence Africaine, Paris, in 1960 under the title *Soundjata ou l'epopee mandinque.*) Reprinted by permission of Longmans, Green, Humanities Press, and Presence Africaine.
6. Basil Davidson, *The Lost Cities of Africa.* Boston: Little, Brown

& Co., 1959, pp. 3-4. Published as *Old Africa Rediscovered* by Victor Gollancz Ltd. Copyright © 1959 by Basil Davidson. Reprinted by permission of Atlantic-Little, Brown & Co. and Victor Gollancz Ltd.

7. Daniel Chu and Elliot Skinner, *A Glorious Age in Africa*. Garden City, New York: Doubleday & Company, Inc., 1965, pp. 87-91, 99-100. Copyright © 1965 by Doubleday and Company, Inc. Reprinted by permission of the publisher.

8. Leon E. Clark and Margaret Morgan, original.

   Basil Davidson, *A Guide to African History*. Garden City, New York: Doubleday & Company, Inc., pp. 29-35. Copyright © 1965 by Doubleday & Company, Inc. Reprinted by permission of Doubleday & Company, Inc.

9. Adapted from William Bosman, *A New and Accurate Description of Guinea*, London, 1705.

   Adapted from C.B. Wadstrom, *Observations on the Slave Trade . . . made in 1787 and 1788 in Company with D.A. Sparrman and Captain Arrhenius*, London, 1789.

10. Olaudah Equiano, *The Interesting Narrative of Olaudah Equiano*, London, 1789, Vol. 1, pp. 3-57, as cited in *Africa Remembered*, Philip D. Curtin, ed. Madison: The University of Wisconsin Press, 1968, pp. 70-78, 85, 88-98.

11. Adapted from Albert J. Swann, *Fighting the Slave Hunters in Central Africa*. Philadelphia: J.B. Lippincott Co., 1910.

12. Basil Davidson, *A History of West Africa 1000-1800*. London: Longmans, Green & Co., 1965, pp. 194-199. U.S. edition: Doubleday Anchor Original, *A History of West Africa to the Nineteenth Century*, New York, 1967, pp. 202-206. Copyright © 1965 Longmans, Green & Co. Ltd. Copyright © 1966 by Basil Davidson. Reprinted by permission of Longmans, Green & Co. Ltd. and Doubleday & Co.

13. Adapted from a report by Robert Craigie, captian of the British ship *Scout*, published in *Papers Relating to Engagements Entered into by King Pepple and the Chiefs of Bonny with her Majesty's Naval Officers on the Subject of the Suppression of the Slave Trade*, 1848.

14. Adapted from the *British and Foreign State Papers*, 1876-1877, Vol. 68, pp. 670-672.

15. Adapted from C.C. Reindorf, *History of the Gold Coast and Asante*. London: Kegan, Paul, Trench, Trubner, 1895, pp. 117-120.

16. Adapted from Henry M. Stanley, *Through the Dark Continent*.

Vol. 2. New York: Harper & Bros., 1885, pp. 268-273.

Remarks of King Mojimba, as told to Father Joseph Fraessle. Reprinted from *The Quest for Africa*, by Heinrich Schiffers, New York: G.P. Putnam's Sons, 1957, pp. 196-197 Copyright © 1957 by G.P. Putnam's Sons. Reprinted by permission of G.P. Putnam's Sons and the Hamlyn Publishing Group Ltd.

17. Adapted from C.N. de Cardi, as reprinted in Mary Kingsley, *West African Studies*, London, 1899, Appendix I, pp. 526-529, 541-545.

18. Chief Kabongo, as told to Richard St. Barbe Baker. From *Kabongo*, by Richard St. Barbe Baker. London: George Ronald, 1955, 107-126. Reprinted by permission of A.S. Barnes & Co. and George Ronald.

19. Adapted from *The Chalmers Report*, Part II, Parliamentary Papers, London, 1899, Vol. 60, pp. 302, 316-317.

20. Stanlake Samkange, *On Trial for My Country*. London: Heinemann Educational Books, 1966, pp. 62-66, 130-134.

21. Richard Harding Davis, *The Congo and Coasts of Africa*. New York: Charles Scribner's Sons, 1907.

22. Colin M. Turnbull, *The Lonely African*. London: Chatto & Windus Ltd.; New York: Simon & Schuster, 1962, pp. 22-27. Copyright © by Colin M. Turnbull. Reprinted by permission of Simon & Schuster and Chatto & Windus Ltd.

23. Colin M. Turnbull, *The Lonely African*. London: Chatto & Windus Ltd.; New York: Simon & Schuster, 1962, pp. 99-108, 110-113. Copyright © 1962 by Colin M. Turnbull. Reprinted by permission of Simon & Schuster and Chatto & Windus Ltd.

24. Chinua, Achebe, *Things Fall Apart*. New York: © 1959 by Chinua Achebe, reprinted by permission of Astor-Honor, Inc., New York, and William Heinemann Ltd.

25. Josiah Strong, *Our Country*, New York, 1885, as quoted in *The Imperialism Reader*, Louis Snyder, ed. Princeton, N.J.: D. Van Nostrand Co., 1962, pp. 122-123. Copyright © 1962, by Litton Educational Publishing, Inc.

26. Tom Mboya, *Freedom and After*. Boston: Little, Brown & Co., 1963, pp. 21-22. Copyright © by Tom Mboya. Reprinted by permission of Little, Brown & Co. and David Higham Associates Ltd.

27. David Diop, "Martyr," in *An Anthology of West African Verse*, Olumbe Bassir, ed. Ibadan, Nigeria: Ibadan University Press, 1957, p. 53. Translated by Olumbe Bassir.

28. James Aggrey, Drum Publications (Proprietory) Ltd. and The

Faith Press, Ltd. as reprinted in *African Nationalisn in the Twentieth Century*, by Hans Kohn, Princeton, N.J.: D. Van Nostrand, 1965, pp. 129-130.

29. Richard Wright, *Black Power*. New York: Harper & Row, 1954, pp. 51-55, 58-60 © 1954 by Richard Wright. Abridged and reprinted by permission of Harper & Row, Publishers, and Paul R. Reynolds, Inc.

30. James Duffy and Robert A. Manners, eds., *Africa Speaks*, New York: Van Nostrand and Reinhold, 1961. Copyright © 1963, Cambridge University Press.

31. D.K. Chisiza, "The Outlook for Contemporary Africa," *The Journal of Modern African Studies*, Vol. I, 1963. Copyright © 1963, Cambridge University Press.

32. Leon Laleau, "Trahison," *Black Orpheus*, Ibaden, Nigeria: Ministry of Education, #2, January, 1958, p. 35. Reprinted by permission of Presence Africaine.

33. David Diop, "Africa" in *A Book of African Verse*, J. Reed and C. Wake, eds. London: Heinemann, 1967, p. 29.

34. L.G. Damas, *Pigments*, Paris: Presence Africaine, 1962, pp. 42-43.

35. Ndabaningi Sithole, *African Nationalism*. London: Oxford University Press, 1962.

36. Donald L. Barnett and Karari Njama, *Mau Mau from Within*. London: Macgibbon & Kee, 1966, pp. 73-75, 118-119, 137-138. Copyright © 1966 by Donald L. Barnett. Reprinted by permission of Granada Publishing Ltd. and Monthly Review Press.

37. James Ngugi, "The Martyr," in *Modern African Prose*, Richard Rive, ed. London: Heinemann, African Writers Series, 1964, pp. 204-214.

38. Kenneth Kaunda, "Some Personal Reflections," in *Africa's Freedom*, London: George Allen & Unwin Ltd., 1964, pp. 24-29, 31-34, 36-37. Reprinted by permission of President Kaunda.

39. Leon E. Clark, original.

Index

Abolition movement, 109, 120
Accra, 212
Achebe, Chinua, 188
African Provincial Council, 266
Age of Exploration, 77
    See also Columbus, Christopher
Aggrey, James, 209
Akhil, Chief, 58
    See also Songhay
Aksum, Ancient Kingdom of
    Ethiopia, 22, 63-74
    See also Ethiopia
Akunna, 188-190
Al Bakri, 29, 33-35
    See also Arab scholars
Algeria, 252
Ali Ber, 57-62
    See also Es-Sadi; Kings; Mali;
    Songhay
Allah, 39
Almammy, King of, 85
Amandebele, 160
Amboko, 179
Angola, 206
Anglo-Saxon, 191-193
Arab
    Scholars
        See Ibn Battuta; Ibn Allah al
    Omani; Albakri
    Slave raiders, 165
    Traders, 30
Armstrong, Louis, 236
Ashanti, 207
Askia Muhammad, 57, 59, 61
    See also Kings; Mali; Songhay

Atheans, 63
Authority, 167-73
Bai Bureh, 149
Balafon, 52
Bambara, 49
    See also Kings
BaNgwana, 187
Barbados, 87, 94
Beecher Report, 248
Belgian Congo
    Casement, Roger, 162
    Colonialism, 119-20, 162-73
    Congo, 162, 66, 201, 221, 222-26
    Leopold, King, 119, 162-66
    Lumumba, Patrice, 221
Belgium, 225
Benin, 132
Berlin, Act of, 166
Berlin Conference, 120, 162
Bias,
    "The Hands of the Blacks,"
        15-18
    in history
    See also Colonialism
Bilad as-Sudan, 27
    See also Western Sudan
Bismarck, Otto von, 119
Black Africa, 212-13
Black Gold, 78
    See also Slavery
Black Jews, 65
    See also Falashas; Religion
Boers, 153
Bolian, 149
Bomanchala, Bo Kama, 54

Bonny, 111-12, 132-33
    King Ja Ja, 132-36
    See also Pepple
Bosman, William, 81
Brandenburghers, 84
Brazil, 109
Britain, See Great Britain
British
    Casement, Roger, 162
    Colonialism, 125-62, 191-94,
        239-63
    Colonies, 272
    Exploration, 125-31
    Rhodes, Cecil, 152-62
    Slave Trade, 78, 80, 87-89, 94,
        104-19
    South Africa Company, 156
    Stanley, Henry, 125-31
Brown, Professor Richard, 233
Buganda, 207
Bushongo, 54-55
Burma, 201
Bwana Jesu, 177, 182-83, 185-86

Cairo, 38-42
Cameroon, 119
Cape of Blanco, 77
Cape of Good Hope, 74
Cardew, Governor, 150
Cardi, C.N. de, 132
Caribbean, 104
Carr, Captain, 149-50
Casement, Roger, 162
Caste system, 61-62
    See also Songhay
Caulknew, W.J., 149
Central Africa, 268, 270
Cesaire, Aime, 235-36
Chalmers, Sir David, 149
Chee, Hee, 110-11
Chibamba, 266
China, 63, 67, 73
Chisiza, Dunduzu Kalui, 227, 235
Christianity, 22, 68, 77-78, 174-87,
    263-64
    See also Missionaries; Religion
Christiansborg, 123

Chukwu, 188-190
Chunyo, 119-121
Churches, see Lalibela
Clark, Leon E., 27, 63
Colonialism, 119-21
    Anti-Colonialism, See United
        Nations
    Berlin Conference, 120, 162, 166
    Christian missionaries, 120, 137,
        174-87
    Colonial expansion, 119-21
    Cultural arrogance, 191-93
    Cultural changes, 167-73
    Dehumanization, 194-97
    Dependency, 131-32, 137
    Education, 167, 174
    Effects of, 131, 148, 162-63,
        194-97
    European motives, 119-121,
        191
    Land Grab, 137-47, 239
    Modernization, 131-32
    Raw materials, need for,
        120, 167
    Scramble for Africa, 119, 207
    Warrant chiefs, 172-73
    White man's burden,
        120-21, 191
Congo
    Lualaba-Congo, 128
    Masoudi, 167-76
    Mellella, King of, 114-15
    River, 114-15, 125
    Republic of, 224
    Slave Trade, 100, See also
        Tip-pu-Tib
    See also Belgian Congo; Zaire
Congolese, 221-22
Convention People's Party (CPP),
    212, 215, 219-20
    Women's Division of, 218
    See also Ghana
Cotton, 167-73
Cowrie, 87
Craigie, Captain Roger, 110-13
Creoles, 148-51
Cuba, 105

See also Sierra Leone
Dances, 233
Danes, 84
Dark Continent, 120, 174
Davis, Richard Harding, 163
Davidson, Basil, 54, 104
Dickens, Charles, 193-93
Dinar, 33
   See also Trade
Diop, David, 194, 196
Do, 52
   See also Kings
Drachma, 41
   See also Egypt
Dugha, 44
Dumas, Leon, 235
"Dumb Barter," 30-32
   See also Silent Trade
Durban, 232
Dutch, 78, 81
   Colonies, 272
   Fraessle, Father Joseph, 125
   Slavery, 80-86, 201
East Africa, 15, 63, 70, 73, 270
   Christianity, 64-74
   Kilwa, 73
   Mozambique, 15
   Tanganyika, 70, 119
   Tanzania, 63, 70, 119, 131
   Trade, 63
   Zimbabwe, 73, 152
   See also Ethiopia
Education, 203
Egypt, 22, 65, 67
   Drachmas, 41
   Independence, 202, 272
   Sultan of, 41
   See also Cairo
Egyptians, 191
Elmina, 82
Empires,
   East Africa, 63-74
   Ghana, 27-36
   Mali, 37-46
   Monomotapa, 232
   Songhay, 57-62
   See also Kingdoms

Equiano, Olaudah, 87, 94
Es-Sadi
   See Ali Ber
Ethiopia, 22, 63-74
   Caste system, 69
   Christianity, 63, 68-69
   Colonialism, 120
   Falashas, 65
   Feudalism, 69
   Independence, 202
   Lalibela, 69
   Selassie, Haile, 63
   Semites, 65
   Sheba, Queen of, 64-65
   Trade, 68, 74-74
   See also Aksum, Ancient Kingdom
     of Ethiopia; Lalibela
Ethnic groups, 208
   Ashanti, 207
   Buganda, 207
   Bushongo, 54-55
   Ewe, 207
   Ibo, 87, 132, 188
   Kamara, 52
   Keitas, 52
   Kikuyu, 137
   Mandingo, 49
   Matebele, 152-61
   Wangara, 29-31, 144
   Yoruba, 207
   Zulu, 207
Ethnocentrism, see Bias
Ewe, 207
Fadama, 52
   See also Kings
Falashas, 65
   See also Ethiopia; Religion
Farma, 150
Fez, 70
Fida, 81-82
   See also Slavery
Firempong, King, 123-24
   See also Kings
Fraessle, Father Joseph, 128
France, 119

French,
Slave Trade, 78, 81, 84-86
French Guiana, 235-36
Fulani,

Gao, 37, 57-58
See also Mali
Gandhi, Mahatma, 213
German, 84
Bismarck, Otto von, 119
Colonization, 119-20
Colonies, 272
Ghana, 206, 209, 232
Ancient, 22, 27-36, 57, 78
Cocoa Trade, 131
"Gold Coast," 78, 104, 206, 209,
219
Independence, 213-20
Kumbi, 29
Nkrumah, Kwame, 212
Soninke, 29
See also West Africa; Warrior
King
Gods
Allah, 39
Bwana Jesu, 177, 182-83, 185-86
Chukwu, 188-90
Ikenga, 188
Kotma, 189
Ngai, 140-41
See also Religion
Gold, 28, 73
Gold Coast, 107, 206, 219
See also Ghana
Great Britain, 270
See also British
Greece, 22, 65
Greeks, 191
Grimm, Jacob, 193
Griots, 47-54
Kouyate, 47
Mali, 47-53
See also Oral Tradition
Grubbe, Sir Hunt, 136
Guimbris, 44
Guinea, 37, 104-08, 206, 220
Guniea Bissau, 206

Haiti, 236
Haley, Alex, 47
See also Oral Tradition
Hebrews, 191
Helm, Rev. Charles D., 154
Hippopotamus Creek, 135
History
Biased, 22
Revised, 24
Holland, 81
See also Dutch
Honwana, Luis Bernado, 15
Hughes, Joseph Elias, 150
Hughes, Miriam Deborah, 150
Human rights, 269-70
Hut Tax War, 148-51
Ibn Battuta, 38, 63
Ibn Fadl Allah al Omari, 38
Ibo, 132, 188
Ibrahimo, 174-88
Ikenga, 188
Imam, 33
See also Muslim; Religion
Impi, 158
Independence
African, general, 202
India, 63-65, 67, 201
Indian Ocean, 70, 73-74
Indians
in Cuba, 105
in West Indies, 105
Industrial Revolution, 109-10, 120
Initiation rites of, 174-187
Slave labor, end of, 109-10
Isaak, 175
Islam
See Religion
Ivory Coast, 78
Ja Ja King, 132-36
Annie Pepple House, 132
in Bonny, 132
Palm oil, 110, 132, 134-35
See also Nigeria
Jameson, 158
Jenne, 21, 43
Johnston, H.H., 136
"Juju," 110, 112

Juju Point, 112 See also Bonny
Kabomp, 149
Kabongo, 137, 143, 145
Kalabi, Lahilatoul, 49
Kamara, 51
Kamp, Nicholas, 123-24
Kasai River, 54
Kassi, Lake, 149
Kaunda, Kenneth, 263
Keitas, 51
   Sundiata Keita, 37, 47
   See also Kings; Mali
Kennedy, President, 263
Kenya, 63, 70, 239, 242, 263
   Independence, 240, 253
   Kenya African Union (KAU),
     244, 246-47
   State of Emergency, 245, 253
   See also Kenyatta, Jomo; Kikuyu;
     Kikuyu Central Association;
     Mau Mau; Mau Mau Revolt
Kenya African Union (KAU), 244,
   246-47
Kenyatta, Jomo, 240-43, 246-47, 250
Keppel, Leicester Chantrey, 114
Keyta, 52
Khartoum, 232
Kikuyu, 137, 234-44
**Kikuyu Central Association
   (KCA),** 244
Kilwa, 63, 70, 73-74
Kimani, 140
Kingdoms,
   Aksum, 63-70
   Ghana, 27-36
   Mali, 37-46, 49-53
   Songhay, 57-62
   Wangara, 29-32
   See also Empires
Kings
   Almammy, 85
   Askia, Muhammad, 57, 59, 61
   Bambara, 49
   Do, 52
   Fadama, 52
   Firempong, 123-24
   Keita, Sundiata, 37, 47

   Leopold of Belgium, 119, 162-
     66
   Lobengula, 152-61
   Mansa Musa, 37-39, 47, 57
   Mellela, 114-15
   Moorish, 84
   Moussa, Fadima, 52
   Selassie, Haile, 63
   Solomon, 64
   Sunni Ali Ber, 57-62
Kipling, Rudyard
   White man's burden, 120-21
   See also Colonialism
Koran (Quran), 46
   See also Muslim
Kotma, 189
Kotokus, 123
Kouyate, Djeli Mamoudou, 47-53
   See also Griots: Kings
Kukya, 61
Kumbi, 29

Lalibela
   Church of, 69
   King Lalibela, 69
"Land of Laughter, The," 231
Language
   Chibamba, 266
   Geez, 68
   "Kitchen kaffir," 266
   Swahili, 70, 74
Lari, 250, 252
Leaders, Nationalist,
   See Chisiza, Dunduzu Kahi;
     Sithole, Ndabaningi
Leopold of Belgium, King, 119,
   162-66
   See also Kings
Liberia, 120, 202
Lincoln, Abraham, 264
Lisbon, 78
Livingston, Stanley, 103
Livingstone, Charles, 135
Livingstonia, 263
Lobengula, King, 152-61
   See also Kings
Lodzi,

See Rhodes, Cecil
Lohali, 129
"Loyalists," African, 244
Lualaba, 128
Lubwa, 263
Luka, Chief of Lari, 250
Lumumba, Patrice, 221
    See also Congo.
Macloutsie, 157-58
Macmillan, Harold, 263
Malawi, 227, 277, 279
Malawi Congress Party, 227
Mali
    Gao, 57
    Griots, 47-53
    Keita, Sundiata, 37, 47
    Mandingo, 49
    Oral Tradition, 47
    Mansa Musa, 37-39, 47, 57
    Songhay, 57-62
    Sunni Ali Ber, 57-62
    Tekrur, 41
    Timbuktu, 57-62
    Tuareg, 58
Mansa Musa, 38-39, 47, 57
    See also Kings; Mali.
Mapelle River, 149
Maputo, 15
Martinique, 235
Mashonaland, 157-60
Masoudi, 167-76
    See also Congo
Matadi, 168, 176-77, 180
Matebele, 153
    See also Ethnic groups.
Matabeleland, 152
Matungi, 169, 172, 180, 185
Mau Mau, 206, 240, 244, 246, 250-51, 253
    Mau Mau movement, 240
    Mau Mau raids, 250-52
    Mau Mau Revolt, 206, 242-45
Mauritania, 194
Mecca
    See Muslim; Religion
Mee, Arthur, 264
Mellella,

Capeta of, 115
King of, 114-15
    See also Kings
Menilik I, 65
Mesopotamia, 236
Middle Ages, 21
Middle East, 65, 67
Missionaries
    Christian, 174-87
    Contributions of, 174
    Dark Continent, 120, 174
    Motives, 120
    Portugal, 77-78
    Prester John, 69, 78
    Strong, Josiah, 191
    Swann, Albert J., 100
    White Fathers, 137
    See also Colonialism
Mission Stations, 263
Mitchell, 165
Mitqal, 33, 42
    See also Trade
Mojimba, Chief, 125, 128
Mokombo, 150
Monomotapa, 232
Moors, 84-85
    See also Kings
Morgan, Margaret, 63
Morocco, 70
Mosques, 68, 70
    See also Muslim; Religion
Moussa, Fadima, 52
    See also Kings
Mozambique, 73, 201, 206
Muezzins, 33
    See also Mulsim; Religion
Mufulira, 265
Mugomo, 145
Mumbi, 248
Munene, 142-44, 146
Muonji, 145
Music
    See Dugha; Balafon; Guimbris
Muslims, 27
    Emir, 39
    Inman, 33

Koran, 46
Mecca, 38
Mosques, 58, 70
Muezzins, 33
See also Arab scholars; Mali; Mansa Musa; Religion; Songhay
Mutanfas, 44
Mysticism, 229
Mzilikazi, 155, 158
Nairobi,
Kenya, 138, 142, 144, 174, 194-96
Massacre in, 257
Naivasha, 250
Namibia, 206
Nationalism, 201, 203, 227, 235;
See also Negritude
Nationalist,
Activities, 207
Movement, 207
See also Kenya African Union; Leaders
Ndola, village of, 167.
See also Congo
Negritude, 235-38
Negres, 223
Negro, 223-24
Negroid, 78
Ngai, 140-41, 147
Niane, D.T., 47
Niger,
People of the, 57
River, 58-59
Nigeria, 35, 87, 132
See also Pepple; Ethnic groups; JaJa, King; Palm oil
Nile, 236
Nkrumah, Kwame, 206, 209, 212-13, 220-21
See also Convention People's Party: Ghana; Independence
Nkumbi, 180-87
Nnanyuki, 246
Normans, 22
Nyasaland, 227, 263.
See also Malawi
Nyerere, Julius, 271
Obi, 188

Ollard, Henry J., 115
Opobo, 133-36
Oral Tradition, 24, 47-53
Haley, Alex, 47
See also Griots.
Oxford University, 152
Palmerston, Lord, 110
Palm Oil, 110, 132, 134-35
Panga, 251
Pepple,
Anna, 110-113
Annie Pepple clan, 132
Annie Pepple House, 132
Bonny, King of, 110
Elloly Pepple, 132
JaJa, King, 132-36
Manilla Pepple House, 133
Pempi, 42-44
Persia, 70
Persian Gulf, 63
Portuguese
Colonies, 272
Exploration, 77-78
Missionaries, 78
Negroids, 78
Prester John, 69-78
Prince Henry, 77
Slave Trade, 78, 80-87, 104-08
Vasco da Gama, 74, 77
Prejudice, See Bias
Prester John, 69, 78
See also Missionaries; Portugal
Pretoria, 280
See also South Africa
Prince Henry, 77
Punt, Land of, 64
See also Ethiopia
Racial segregation, 212
Reindorf, C.C., 123
Religion,
Black Jews, 65
Christianity, 68, 77-78, 174-87, 263-74
Islam, 60-61, 74
Reporter Magazine, 174-88
Republic of South Africa,
See South Africa

Rhodes, Cecil, 152-61
Rhodesia, 152-61
　Northern Rhodesia, 263-64
　　See also Zambia
　Southern Rhodesia, 206
　　See also Zimbabwe
Rights of man, declaration of, 224
Rogers, Andrew W., 115
Romans, 63, 65, 67, 122, 191
Rudd, Charles D., 152
Russia, 270
　See also Soviet Union
Sabeans, 65
Samkange, Stanlake, 153
Sankore, University of, 58-59
Sankuru, 54
Schiffers, Heinrich, 125
Scotland, Church of, 263
Selassie, Haile, 63, 65, 69
　See also Ethiopia
Semites, 65
　Israelites, 65
　Sabeans, 65
　See also Ethiopia
Senegal, 27, 37, 201, 236
　French slave trade, 84-86
　River, 30, 84
　Senegal Company, 85
　See also Negritude
Senghor, Leopold Sedar, 235-36
　See also Nationalism; Negritude;
　Senegal
Seven Years War, 87
Sheba, Queen of, 64-65
Sierra Leone, 148-51
Silent Trade, 30
　See also "Dumb Barter"
Sithole, Rev. Ndabaningi, 202, 240
　See also Zimbabwe
Slaves
　African, 80
　Children, 100-03
　Condition of, 100-03
　"Invalides," 82
　Price of, 83
　Sale of, 81-83
　Separation from relatives, 87-93

　See also Slave Trade
Slave Trade, 104-08
　Abolition movement, 109, 120
　African
　American plantations, 104
　Ammunition, guns, 80-81, 83-
　　84
　Arab, 165
　Black gold, 78
　British, 109-11
　Caravans, 100-03,
　　See also Tip-pu-Tib
　Chicote, 102
　Demand for labor, 104-08
　Ending of, 109-13
　Effect on Africa, 100
　Fida, 81-82
　Forced march technique, 101-03
　Forces of, 78, 104-08
　Internecine wars, 80-86
　Ivory, 101-03
　Portuguese, 78, 81
　Private, 85
　Public, 85
　Slave wars, 100
　Spanish, 104-08
　Treaties, 114-15
　Treatment, 87-99
　Triangular Trade, 104-08
　West African, 81
　West Indies, 104-08
　See also Bosman, William; British;
　　Dutch; French; Portuguese
Smith, Adam, 109
Solar Eclipse, 55-56
Solomon, King, 64-65
　See also Kings
Somalia, 208
Somalis, 208
Songhay, 57-62
　Akhil, Chief, 58
　Ammar, 58
　Army, 61-62
　Askia Muhammad, 57-61
　Caste system, 61-62
　Sunni Ali Ber, 57-58, 62
　Timbuktu, 57-62